VOLUME 13 / PART 2

Edited by **Grace Emmerson and John Parr**

The Bible Reading Fellowship
OPENING THE BIBLE

Writers in this issue

The Holy Spirit   **Tom Smail** was prominent in the charismatic renewal in the 1970s (he was Director of the Fountain Trust until 1979). He taught at St John's, Nottingham from 1979 to 1985 and was a Team Rector in South Croydon until his retirement in 1994. He is the author of a number of books, including *Reflective Glory* and *The Forgotten Father*.

Deuteronomy   **Professor Ronald Clements** trained for the Baptist ministry after a spell as a bank clerk and in National Service. He has spent most of his working life teaching Old Testament in British universities—Edinburgh, Cambridge and London (King's College). He is well known as a writer and is interested in drawing the devotional and intellectual aspects of Bible study closer together.

Acts   **E. Margaret Embry** was for many years a tutor/lecturer in New Testament Studies at Trinity College, Bristol. She is now retired, but continuing ministry in South Bristol.

Nahum and Obadiah   **Dr Rex Mason** served as a Baptist minister in churches in West Ham, Upminster and Cardiff before becoming Tutor in Old Testament at Spurgeon's College, London, and later Tutor and Fellow in Old Testament and Hebrew at Regent's Park College, Oxford, and Lecturer in the University of Oxford. He is currently President of the Society for Old Testament Study.

Hebrews   **Claire Amos** has lived and taught biblical studies in Jerusalem, Beirut and Cambridge, to both clergy and laity. Currently she is editor of Partners in Learning, an ecumenical journal which provides resources for all-age worship. She also lectures in Old and New Testament at the Roehampton Institute in South London, and to ordinands in Kent.

Jesus and Prayer   **John Parr** is Priest in Charge of Harston and Hauxton near Cambridge, and Director of Continuing Ministerial Education in the Ely Diocese. He is joint-editor of *Guidelines*.

1 Samuel   **Dr Stephen Dawes** is Chairman of the Cornwall District of the Methodist Church. Formerly he taught Old Testament and Hebrew at Trinity College, Legon, Ghana and at Queen's College, Birmingham.

Editors' Letter

The beginning of this issue coincides with the approach of Pentecost. To prepare us for this great festival, Tom Smail, a new contributor to *Guidelines*, has written a short series of notes on the Holy Spirit. These are followed by Ronald Clements' readings in Deuteronomy, a work of urgent exhortation which also brings out the joy of living close to God—a strong Pentecost theme. Margaret Embry takes up the story of the Acts of the Apostles at the point where the early Church began to make inroads into the Gentile world. The familiarity and accessibility of the New Testament writing is in marked contrast with what at first sight appears to be the harsh and uncongenial message of Nahum and Obadiah. Rex Mason skilfully helps us to appreciate their splendid poetry and to perceive their challenge for today. The notes on Hebrews are not what we originally planned. We had intended to publish four weeks of readings, but the person we commissioned had to pull out at the last minute because of serious family illness. So we are re-publishing Clare Amos' excellent notes from 1992. Because these run for three weeks, a week of readings on 'Jesus and Prayer' have been added, to suggest some possible connections between the message of Hebrews and the teaching of Jesus. The issue finishes with notes on 1 Samuel 1–16. The stories here make exciting reading, but their relevance to Christian readers is not always obvious. Stephen Dawes draws on his fine sense of narrative to show that they do not simply tell a good story, but make a powerful affirmation of God at work in human lives.

Thank you for your letters—one from a reader in South Africa who has been using BRF notes for 55 years. Well done! Thanks also to the reader who responded to the notes on the Song of Songs in a past issue with a delightful little composition of his own!

We are sometimes asked why the week's notes start on Monday. Are we simply copying the practice of some modern diaries? The answer is 'no': Sunday is emphatically the first day of the week. Some of our readers tell us that they use the specially appointed lectionary readings for Sunday as part of their preparation for Sunday worship. By following the suggested dating, the 'Guidelines' section on Sundays can be used as a way of reflecting on the way the word of God has addressed the week's work and activity. But there is no reason why you should not start the notes on Sundays if you wish. The important thing is to adapt *Guidelines* to your particular circumstances.

If you enjoy *Guidelines* and find it helpful in your Christian pilgrimage, why not introduce it to a friend? You could send a copy using the form on page 157.

With all good wishes

Grace Emmerson, John Parr

The BRF Prayer

O God our Father,
in the holy scriptures
you have given us your word
to be our teacher and guide:
help us and all the members of our Fellowship
to seek in our reading
the guidance of the Holy Spirit
that we may learn more of you
and of your will for us,
and so grow in likeness to your Son,
Jesus Christ our Lord.
Amen.

THE BRF
Magazine

Richard Fisher writes...

Thank you for all your letters! During recent months we have received dozens of letters telling how and why BRF Bible reading notes are special to you—from some for whom BRF notes provided a spiritual lifeline during the Second World War, either as prisoners of war, or serving in the armed forces far from home; from some who were first introduced to the notes as a child and have read them literally for decades now; and letters from many who have found that God has spoken very clearly to them through the notes during a particular crisis or experience.

Thank you also for all your kind comments about *New Daylight* and *Guidelines*, and about *The BRF Magazine*. We are delighted that so many of you see it as a welcome addition to each issue.

Disciple

In the last issue of the *Magazine* you will have read about *Disciple*, a new initiative which is now available in the UK through a partnership between The Foundery Press and BRF. *Disciple* is a 34-session course which provides a framework for people to relate the teaching of the Bible to their discipleship today. Already many churches have sent leaders to the special three-day training seminar to learn about how to implement and teach the *Disciple* course in their churches, and *Disciple* groups are being established throughout the UK. If you

would like further details about this exciting initiative and what it might offer to your church or fellowship, send an A4 31p s.a.e. clearly marked 'Disciple' in the top left hand corner to BRF in Oxford.

Livewires and The People's Bible Commentary

These two major new resources are now available from BRF and are being very well received. We first mentioned them both in the September 1996 issue of the *Magazine* and launched them in October 1996.

Livewires is the cornerstone of our Bible reading resources for 7–10 year olds and is published under our children's imprint *Barnabas*. Look out for the Barny logo for quality children's resources from BRF. There will be 18 titles in the *Livewires* range, together providing a comprehensive introduction to the people, places and events of the Bible, along with a range of themes relating the Bible to everyday Christian life. *Livewires* is also available on subscription, and can be ordered regularly along with your *New Daylight* and *Guidelines* notes. For further details see page 157.

The People's Bible Commentary will eventually cover every book of the Bible, creating a complete library of readable commentaries which address both head and heart—deepening our understanding of the text, and enabling us to worship and pray in response to what we read. Each Bible book is divided into a number of passages and for each passage there is a double page spread of commentary and a prayer. You can therefore work through each book systematically and on a daily basis if you wish. A voucher scheme enables you to collect a voucher from each volume which counts towards further free copies. Full details are included on the last page of each commentary.

Our hope and prayer is that both these new resources will serve to draw even more readers into a deeper awareness of and relationship with God through the Bible and through prayer. If we can achieve that, then we are fulfilling the objective and vision for which BRF was brought into being 75 years ago.

BRF Representatives

As a regular reader of BRF notes you will no doubt be aware of our network of many thousands of Group Secretaries who are responsible for ordering and distributing BRF Bible reading notes to readers in their church(es). We are enormously indebted to them all for the hard work and support which they give to BRF year after year.

As we celebrate our 75th Anniversary we should like to expand this network further. If you would like details of how you could become a BRF Group Secretary in your church, or if you know someone who might be interested, please let us know.

Alongside the Group Secretary network, we are seeking to develop a network of BRF Representatives, who will promote the work of BRF as a whole (the resources, the charitable work, the vision) at a local level, building links with churches, holding book parties and events. If you are looking for a challenge and would like to become involved with BRF in this way, please contact Karen Laister here at the BRF office for further details.

Special Projects News

In the last two issues I have written of our support of ministers in Papua New Guinea, to whom we have sent BRF books. Recently a letter arrived from our main contact there, who wrote: 'We were delighted to learn of the wonderful response to the Fellowship's appeal for aid for supporting churches. We are thrilled by your news that such a large consignment of books is on its way to us... Please thank all members of the Fellowship for their support. Priests here, and Pastors the world over, must be deeply indebted to you all for providing much needed tools for Bible study, with flocks who cannot afford to buy such books as you provide.'

There is such an urgent need for those in ministry and with responsibility for teaching and preaching to be equipped properly for Bible study themselves if they are to be effective in their leadership. If you can help us to send more BRF Bible study books to those in countries like Papua New Guinea, where they either have little access to or cannot afford such resources, please do consider supporting this work. Every donation counts, no matter how large or small, and will enable us to develop this initiative further.

Romania

You will have read also in previous issues of our support for a project in Romania to help the Romanian Evangelical Society to produce a version of *New Daylight* in Romanian, combining notes translated from our own edition with those specially written by Romanian Christians themselves. This project was initially for three six-month editions, but was then extended to include a one year volume. The project has now come to an end in terms of BRF providing financial support (some £12,000 during the last three years), but we will continue to provide material from *New Daylight* for translation for the Romanian edition.

75th Anniversary

Our 75th Anniversary year continues and on page 9 you will find details of events still to come during 1997. Please do write and let us know if you are planning or have already held any special events of your own to mark this BRF milestone. And if there is anything we can do to help, do ask! For example we know of one church which is also celebrating its 75th Anniversary during the Autumn and so we are discussing plans for a joint celebration with them.

Christian Resources Exhibition

If you live within reach of Esher, Surrey, do come and visit us at the annual Christian Resources Exhibition (20–23 May 1997) at Sandown Park. Several BRF authors, including Adrian Plass, will be visiting the Exhibition and spending time with us on the BRF stand each day. BRF authors will also be involved in the extensive lecture programme. The Christian Resources Exhibition is well worth a visit—if you have never been before, why not make this year your first?

75th Anniversary Update

To remind you of what is happening and give you new information regarding events and initiatives for the remainder of the year...

Group Secretary Day

The final Group Secretary Day will take place on 13 September. If you are a Group Secretary you should already have received details of this. If you have not had these, please let us know as soon as possible.

Christian Resources Exhibitions

Come and meet BRF authors and staff, find out more about the work of the Fellowship and see the latest new publications.

20–23 May 1997
Sandown Park, Esher, Surrey

23–25 October 1997
G-MEX, Manchester.

Bible Sunday

Full details of the outline service, drawing from the Service of Thanksgiving and Rededication (which was held on 30 January), will be available in the next issue of the *Magazine*.

Author Tour

We can now announce that our author tour in October will be with Adrian Plass, whose new book will be published by BRF that month. Final details of dates and venues will be published in the next issue of the *Magazine*, but if you wish to have the information earlier, please send an A5 20p s.a.e. clearly marked 'Plass Tour' in the top left hand corner to BRF in Oxford.

Information Pack

This is still available, containing ideas and suggestions for what you might do in your own church or area to celebrate BRF's anniversary and to promote and encourage Bible reading. Contact the BRF office to request your copy.

Souvenir Brochure

This will be available to all readers of the notes during the latter part of the year and will include the story of how BRF came into being. Details of how you may obtain your copy will be included in the next issue of the *Magazine*.

Profile of The Rt Revd Patrick Harris

The Right Reverend Patrick Harris is the Bishop of Southwell and also the Chairman of the Bible Reading Fellowship's Council.

He has been married to Valerie since 1968, and they have three grown-up children. Jonathan, who is a teacher at Dean Close School; David, who works in Boots; and Rachel, who, after taking a degree in anthropology, is now doing a Post-Graduate Certificate of Education at Oxford Brookes University.

Patrick Harris spent most of his childhood in St Alban's and went to St Alban's School. After doing his two years' national service with the Royal Artillery in Germany he read law at Oxford. Before going to Keble College, Oxford, a friend asked him a question which changed the course of his life.

> *'Do your best to present yourself to God as one approved, a workman who has no need to be ashamed, rightly handling the word of truth.'*

'He challenged me as to whether God might not be calling me into the ministry,' Patrick Harris told me. 'Wham.' With the realization that God was indeed calling him, he went through the selection process and eventually did his theological training in Bristol at Clifton Theological College.

His first job was as curate to The Revd Basil Gough at St Ebbe's Church in Oxford. Then for the next seventeen years he was in Argentina, serving with the South American Missionary Society. 'I was working with the Mataco Indians', he told me, 'and I am bilingual in Mataco and in Spanish.' He still has a great interest in South American, particularly

Indian, culture. 'I am going back to Argentina for a week in October', he said. 'I have been a member of the South Atlantic Council which has sought to bridge-build after the Falklands War between the two countries. I will be a delegate in the Argentine–British Conference which is held annually.'

Patrick Harris likes reading—and biographies are particular favourites. 'At the moment I'm reading an exhaustive biography of Cranmer, who was a son of Nottinghamshire, by Diarmaid MacCulloch' he said, 'and another on Jorge Luis Borges, *The Man in the Mirror of the Book*. He was an Argentine novelist and poet who had a worldwide influence.' Another pleasure is a wide variety of music. 'I particularly enjoy Bach, Mozart and Schubert,' he told me, 'and opera and ballet.'

I wanted to know why, in a busy and demanding life as a Bishop, he was prepared to give the time to be involved with the BRF as Chairman of its Council, and why he thinks it is a good organization. This is what he told me:

'From the very earliest days as a Christian, a friend, Richard Hovil, taught me about the vital importance of the Word of God in daily life. And he gave me a verse which I have never forgotten—2 Timothy 2:15.

' "Do your best to present yourself to God as one approved by him, a worker who has no need to be ashamed, rightly explaining the word of truth" (NRSV).

'I am greatly concerned about the lack of daily Bible reading amongst Christians. And I want to do all that I can to encourage it, both in our nation and in other countries. As we draw near to the millennium Christians need to be strengthened and inspired to take forward the cause of God's kingdom and the Good News of Jesus Christ. And BRF is one of the best agencies to do this.'

Shelagh Brown

'As we draw near to the millennium Christians need to be strengthened and inspired to take forward the cause of God's kingdom and the Good News of Jesus Christ.'

Profile of Robert Aldred

Robert Aldred is a teacher at St Edward's School in Oxford. He is also a member of the BRF Council and Executive Committee, and he is Chairman of BRF's Publications Committee.

He and his wife, Alison, have three grown-up children: Sophie, Clare and James.

Robert Aldred has been at St Edward's School for twenty-four years, eleven of them as a House Master of Field House. He was brought up in Reigate, Surrey, and went to school at St Lawrence, Ramsgate. At Durham University he did English, Latin and psychology. 'My first job was teaching in a small school for people with learning difficulties,' he told me, 'in the days before that was usual, and I followed that by teaching at St Lawrence for five years before moving to St Edward's.'

In the sixties Robert was on the team of the Scripture Union Beach Mission at Sheringham (what used to be known as the CSSM), and for four years in the late seventies he was the leader of the team. 'It was great to lead a talented group of young people who were keen to share their faith with others', he

> *'It was great to lead a ... group of young people who were keen to share their faith.'*

said. 'I even took Ali there at the end of our honeymoon and we ended up spending five days there because the team was shortstaffed!'

Alison trained as a nurse, and for some years after they moved to Oxford she worked in the student clinic at University College. It was there that she and Robert met the Chaplain, Bill Sykes, and it was through them that BRF has been able to publish Bill's unique series of *Visions* books. Alison now works as a chiropodist, visiting people in their houses. They live in Weston-on-the-Green, which has been put on the map because that is where the tennis star Tim Henman comes from.

Robert teaches English and Divinity. He also teaches a General Studies Course in Theology and another in Ethics in the Lower and Upper Sixth. In those courses he makes liberal use of Bill Sykes' *Visions* books, which he finds remarkably effective. He helps coach the hockey and also runs the golf at St Edward's. 'I have always had a great interest in sport,' he said, 'and in my more athletic days I was a very keen hockey player and a cricketer. But now I have moved to golf!'

One of his passions is ornithology. 'I birdwatch all the time, even when I'm in the car—much to the annoyance of the family! I've seen red kite flying over the Chilterns—and they are the most marvellous, wonderful creatures. Some pairs were released in the Chilterns and in recent weeks one has been seen flying over Weston. It is my hope that this beautiful bird, which has been persecuted to the point of near extinction, can be re-established in this country. It used to be common over the whole of the British Isles, in the country and in the towns, and it does no harm at all to the human world or to the world of farming. Yet people shoot it and kill it. It feeds on carrion and it's a cleaner-upper of the countryside. It never kills animals itself. But when people put down poison for rabbits it kills the red kite.'

As well as bird watching Robert likes to read. 'But I do it in spurts,' he told me, 'mostly during the holidays. I have just read a wonderful book—*The Railwayman*. It's a marvellous story of forgiveness and a 'must' for everybody. It's about a man who was a prisoner-of-war in Burma and for fifty years sustained a burning hatred for one of his guards. But over those years that same guard had a burning desire for reconciliation—and then, after fifty years, they met.'

I asked Robert to tell me about his connection with BRF. 'I've found it a fascinating challenge,' he said, 'and it has come at exactly the right time of my life, just after spending eleven years as a housemaster. It is a great opportunity to be involved with something which is outside the school and which is so interesting, and I hope that I can bring something of my experience as a schoolmaster into the work at BRF. What is fascinating, too, is the way in which BRF is developing as an organization. It isn't simply that it is publishing more books now than it ever has in the past, but it really has a sense of mission—to serve the churches and to help them and resource them with the material that it is producing. And the way it is all developing is very, very interesting.'

Shelagh Brown

> *'BRF really has a sense of mission—to serve the churches and to help them and resource them.'*

13

The Poise of Grace: Life 'in Christ'

Simon Barrington-Ward

It's difficult to recall now that strange period in the sixties when so many young seekers 'dropped out' from their education, or from the 'rat race' into which they felt it led, and set off in search of fulfilment in the mysterious East. So often their hopes came to grief in India or Pakistan, or somewhere on the famous 'trail' to Kabul.

1. The *Dilaram* community

I remember one young man (I'll call him Andrew) for whom this happened. He collapsed in a youth hostel in Delhi. Disappointed by a variety of would-be *gurus* he had taken to drugs and picked up some infection from a dirty needle. So it was that he ended up by being brought into what was called the *Dilaram* community, *dilaram* being the Hindi word for peace.

This was a place where he immediately felt welcomed, cherished and cared for. The rooms were clean, shady, colour-washed in soft tones. They were set in thick walls and cooled by fans. Those who floated round looking after him, European and Asian, men and women, looked like fellow hippies, clad in robes or saris of similar colours to those on the walls.

It soon became clear from the icons around those walls and from the prayers and songs of worship with which they echoed that those who dwelt within them were Christian, in a way which Andrew found attractive and deeply sustaining. A small group of them nursed him through his fever and then through the terrible sensation of being released from the grip of heroin.

Gradually, in this setting, he came to feel strangely comforted and comfortable at every level of his consciousness, physical, emotional and spiritual, as though in some deeply underlying area of himself, he had genuinely 'come home'.

But quite soon there was another awareness dawning on him. Most of those who cared for him were fellow casualties. Even the permanent 'members' were the same. And every one was expected to do the housework and the chores as soon as they could. That, as in all community life, was where the working out of his new peace began. Having been 'given', it now also had to be won. And yet, over all, what you encountered here was always, first and foremost, a culture of acceptance. That sense of mutual forgiveness and for-given-ness was always primary.

Within its security you could then also find yourself being confronted with your own selfishness, idle-ness or resentfulness, and coming up against those same tendencies in others, in ways which could be painful. And yet again, even through that sharp encounter, the implicit invitation to admit your own fault was always present. And with this admission, you kept breaking through once more to an even deeper and more far-reaching affirmation of your own value and a release of your gifts in a way which was profoundly healing and help-ful.

At the heart of this continuing rhythm of repentance and forgive-ness lay shared prayer and worship. Those times of waiting on the pres-ence and love of God together were increasingly central to the common

At the heart of this continuing rhythm of repentance and forgiveness lay shared prayer and worship.

life of *Dilaram* as Andrew experi-enced it. From such interludes there flowed a wider awareness that the action of grace was setting in motion a continuous breaking and remaking, not only in one's inner self, not only in the life of the com-munity, but in the world at large.

It was for Andrew, as for all of those with him, to be part of that breaking and remak-ing, both by his prayer and in his whole way of living. He was to go out from there committed to this redemptive process in the world around him, in what-ever job he found himself called to, in the building of friend-ships, of future mar-riage and family per-haps, in social action in politics, in the struggle for justice, for true human community, for the preservation of the planet itself from destruction. For Andrew the quest was no longer so much for a way of being, as for a way of *becoming*.

2. A way of becoming

The source, the theme and the goal of this shared way of life into which Andrew had now entered was 'Christ'. That is to say that from the very beginning the love which was communicated to him as he lay sick in the room to which he had been

15

brought so thankfully, was the love of God, brought home to us all in the person of Jesus Christ.

The teaching of Jesus, his activity, his taking of our burdens upon him in his suffering and death, and the shared, risen life which he opened up to his disciples, through the power of the Spirit he breathed into them: these were the realities constantly informing the whole development of *Dilaram*. They led into a kind of living out of one's baptism together with others, a shared life, a rhythm of constant entering in upon Christ's death and resurrection, of continual rebirth.

'I press on to grasp that for which Christ has already grasped me'

For each and all of us, as for the whole universe, this was a 'way', a journey within which we have already arrived at our goal 'in Christ', as Andrew did when he entered the very door of *Dilaram*, and yet we are also still not there, still, while this world lasts, journeying 'in hope'.

3. The Pauline balance

The realism and the scope of this universal way of becoming are well caught by St Paul, both in Romans chapter 8 and, more personally perhaps, in Philippians chapters 3 and 4. He speaks of being held himself in what appears to be a marvellous balance, poised, like the creation itself, between having arrived and still travelling.

'Not as though I have already attained, or have yet reached perfection, but I press on to grasp that for which Christ has already grasped me' (Philippians 3:12). This is the poise, not of confidence in our own achievement, but of trust, of faith in that love which in Christ has taken hold of us and will freely, with him, in the end give us everything. It is faith which knows 'both how to be abased and how to abound', trusting in that grace, which enables Paul to say, 'I can do all things through Christ which strengthens me' (Philippians 4:12–13).

Nowhere else can there be found quite such a fusion of both failure and hope; commitment to a fully this-worldly life and yet power to reach through and beyond it; a fusion of honesty and vulnerable humility on the one hand and yet of the release of transforming gifts and love on the other. It is here—within the life that flows from trust in the person and cross and resurrection of Christ—that not only Andrew but all of us, and the whole universe of which we are a part, can find a way of becoming, a way that opens up into a new and boundless creation yet to be!

Abusing God's Creation

An extract from Time to Change by Hugh Montefiore

A horrible new strain of the rare Creutszfeldt-Jakob Disease (CJD) in humans has appeared in the last twelve years. It seems to attack younger people, and it takes less time to develop. The sufferer gradually loses his memory, sinks into a coma, and dies. There is no cure.

No one has actually proved as yet a link with Mad Cow Disease (BSE) but it seems probable from experiments with other animals. Most people think that the epidemic of BSE, now ten years old, was caused by a special type of cattle feed, which has also been used as fertiliser on cattle pastures. This was particularly rich in protein because it included the ground up remains of both cattle and sheep.

Some sheep have long been infected by a similar illness called Scrapie (non infectious to humans). Experts believe that the infection has now jumped from one species to another. Scrapie, they think, has become BSE in cattle through the cattle feed and grass they have eaten, and BSE

Herbivores have unwittingly been turned into carnivores, even cannibals.

has become CJD in humans through their eating infected beef. These illnesses take a long time to develop, so no one can tell whether we shall suffer a huge epidemic of CJD or there will be only a few more cases. To prevent future infection, thousands of cattle have to be burnt. Until this is done, no one overseas wants to buy our beef. The beef industry is in ruins.

Cattle naturally eat only grass. If this is the origin of CJD, it has been caused by making them consume feed which contains remains of cattle and sheep. Herbivores have unwittingly been turned into carnivores, even cannibals. This shows a gross lack of respect for animals which we human beings have domesticated.

It offends against the natural law of their being. It is a horrible offence for which, it seems, we may be horribly punished.

We have to ask ourselves whether we are treating the natural world today in such a way that we are in danger of bringing upon ourselves not blessings but a curse. God does not strike us directly; but he has so designed the natural world that if we do not respect its proper boundaries, the results rebound upon ourselves. This is one of the spiritual truths to be found in the famous story of Adam and Eve. They were in charge of the Garden of Eden, but they disobeyed the rules of their stewardship. As a result they found that this disobedience rebounded on themselves. 'Cursed is the ground because of you; in toil you shall eat of it all the days of your life' (Genesis 3:17).

It would be wrong to imagine that the curses mentioned in Deuteronomy were all literally fulfilled. But the Old Testament prophets insist that the Jews lost their inheritance in the Holy Land because they had not kept the commandments of God. These commandments were not for the most part concerned with the environ-

If we disobey the natural laws of God, we must expect the judgment of God to come upon us.

ment, or with cattle in particular. After all, they were spoken to the children of Israel in a very different situation thousands of years ago.

In those days no one could imagine that they were harming the environment. Much time was taken up in trying to ensure that the environment did not harm them. But the principle holds: if we disobey the natural laws of God, we must expect the judgment of God to come upon us. And this is what is happening today. We are abusing it, and suffering judgment as a result. Some of the correspondences are striking. 'Cursed shall be the increase of your cattle and the young of your flock.' That is precisely what many people today must be thinking about Mad Cow Disease.

'Cursed shall you be in the city' we read. We are prepared to tolerate terrible conditions in our inner cities, and in the favelas and shanty towns of huge conurbations in other countries. The result? Huge increases in crime. For many it has indeed become a curse to live in such places.

'Cursed be the fruit of your body.' Well, not yet; but the mysterious drop in sperm count will affect birth rates if not stemmed. No one is certain what causes it. Some think it is due to the use of chemicals with particles which mimic elements in the human reproductive system. These chemicals are abroad in the environment, and may threaten not merely human reproduction, but that of animals as well.

As for the threat of diseases, this is all but upon us now, with a new deadly strain of staphylococcus which hospitals find so hard to eradicate and which only one antibiotic can touch. It seems the prodigal and unnecessary use of antibiotics has produced this new type of bacterium. In a rather similar way, patients who did not finish their course of TB treatment have brought about a new airborne strain of this disease which, it is said, is likely to kill thirty million people in the next decade...

In the Bible readings and comments that follow we shall be exploring these and other matters in greater detail. We shall be contrasting our present practices with biblical principles. In the past the Church has been reluctant to concern itself with the environment. Our Christian leaders have not been warning us, and lay Christians have not been in the forefront of the battle.

REFLECT AND PRAY

Two thousand years ago Jesus called people to follow him. He calls them still. He gave his first disciples tasks to do. He gives us tasks to do today. He told them to proclaim God's kingly rule, and to share in it. He calls us to do the same. He called people to a change of heart. He calls us too.

Reflect that the risen Christ is always with us. His call to us is as real as it was to Peter and Andrew, and James and John. Then perhaps pray these prayers, or a different prayer of your own.

Jesus, I want to follow you all the days of my life. Show me what you want, and I will do it, with your help.

O God, please show me what I can do to help to restore the environment of your world. Help me to a change of heart, help me to understand, to see clearly and to think clearly. Amen

He told them to proclaim God's kingly rule, and to share in it. He calls us to do the same.

***

Time to Change is available from your local Christian bookshop or, in case of difficulty, direct from BRF. See the order form on page 159 for details.

Look out for BRF's brand new confirmation course for young people:

CONNECTING WITH GOD
A young person's guide to believing and belonging

If you are responsible for running the Confirmation or Church membership group for young people in your church then *Connecting With God* is for you.

In ten practical and thought-provoking sessions this book aims to get young people thinking about who they are, why the Christian faith is so important, and where they're going in connection with God.

Designed to help young people think for themselves and make up their own minds about life's most important decision, *Connecting With God* looks at the biblical basis of the Christian faith and its implications for young people as individuals within the context of their local church.

Jude Levermore's practical and innovative approach to preparing young people for Confirmation has been warmly welcomed by the young people in her own church. Her tried and tested ideas make this book an ideal resource for all young people wanting to know more about connecting with God, whichever church they belong to.

Jude is a course tutor at Oxford Youth Works, which has gained an excellent reputation in relational

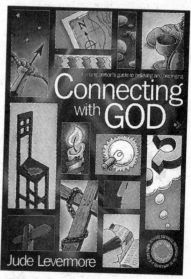

youthwork, both in its work with young people and in training others to do it. She is also a Director of Greenbelt Festivals and a Lay Reader in the Diocese of Oxford. She is joint author of *Youthwork and How To Do It*, published by Lynx Communications.

Connecting with God is illustrated by popular cartoonist Simon Smith.

Photocopy permission is included for all worksheet and diary pages which are designed to be built up week by week as a permanent record of the young person's reflections on the course.

Connecting With God takes you through:

 Connecting with Each Other

 Connecting with God the Creator

 Connecting with God the Son

Connecting with God the Holy Spirit

 Connecting with God the Father

Connecting with the Bible

 Connecting with Prayer

Connecting with the Church

 Confirming the Connection

Keeping up the Connection

Each session includes:

 PREPARATION AND SESSION AIM
gets you prepared and focused

 FIRST CONNECTIONS
gets your group prepared and focused

BIBLE CONNECTIONS
explores the session theme through the Bible

 FURTHER CONNECTIONS
expands the teaching

 CONNECTING WITH GOD
explains the teaching

 THE BIG QUESTION
puts the point across

 CONCLUDING CONNECTIONS
draws it together
PERSONAL CONNECTIONS SHEET
(with photocopy permission)
group worksheets and diary pages for individual use by each member of your group

As well as being an excellent foundational introduction to the Christian faith and an ideal preparation for Confirmation, this course also provides you, as a leader in your church, with the springboard for an on-going building of relationships with young people.

All BRF's resources for young people aim to help children in the 11+ age group to explore the Christian faith in the context of their own life experience. We hope that you'll find this exciting course a worthwhile tool in helping your young people to grow towards God.

Connecting with God is available from your local Christian bookshop or, in case of difficulty, direct from BRF. See page 159 for details.

Prayer for all Seasons (1)

Joy Tetley

His scream pierced the eerie and untimely darkness. The state's machinery of torture had yet again proved effective. Human gifts of ingenuity and intelligence once more put to the service of inflicting maximum human suffering. Like many before and since, this dying victim was paying the price of standing for truth, where truth proved too threatening.

Like many before and since, this figure crying into the dark was enduring an agony he most certainly did not deserve.

The pain of his execution was compounded by the triumphant taunts of those who wanted rid of him—and had got their way. The words he shouted were difficult to distinguish; distorted, almost throttled by the suffocating pressure on his body. Some, taking perverse pleasure in the event, misheard. But somehow (though this man had been abandoned by his closest friends) true witness emerged—and came to be recorded.

> *This figure crying into the dark was enduring an agony he most certainly did not deserve.*

'My God, my God, why hast thou forsaken me?' Utter desolation. Incomprehension. Determined faithfulness betrayed: not only by human associates but also, it seemed, by God.

Here is prayer at its most basic, raw and elemental. Here, thrown at an absent God, is a question at the heart of human experience: Why? Why? (Not for nothing did Bach emphasize and repeat that word in his *Matthew Passion*). And here is a question that comes straight from the heart of Jesus—right from the core of his being and out of the middle of his desperate situation. The luxury of distanced debate is a million miles away.

Contemplate Jesus, urges the writter of the Epistle to the Hebrews. Look to Jesus. 'See' Jesus. For in so doing, you will see the truth about yourself, the truth about humankind and—most amazingly of all—the truth about God.

It is the claim of Hebrews (and, indeed, of Christians down the ages) that Jesus is the self-expression of God in human form. Looking to Jesus means seeing into the life and character of God. What that implies about God is staggering.

It means that the God who is, by definition, greater than the mysterious immensity of the universe, the God who is source and energy of all creation, this God knows from the inside what it means to be human; knows joy and love and hope and yearning; knows laughter and tears, vitality and weariness; knows fulfilment and frustration, wellbeing and suffering; knows compelling visions and shattered dreams, utter commitment and (from others) radical rejection.

And somehow, this God even knows what it is like to feel God-forsaken, to feel totally alone. There, truly, is humanity's most profound source of hope. God knows! Hidden in that popular expletive is the Word made flesh. So often we know not what we say. We utter transforming truth, and translate it into empty words.

But truth remains. Truth waits to be discovered. Truth longs to take hold of us for good. For truth is, essentially and eternally, personal and passionate. When we look, openly, to Jesus, such truth is disclosed. We find someone 'like us'; we find someone who can meet us where we are (in every sense of that phrase). We find someone who can go with us, even through hell. We find someone who can encourage, strengthen and challenge us to the roots, someone who can draw out of us what we hardly realized we had it in us to be. We find God.

In Jesus, too, we see humanity as it could and should be. And in Jesus we discover the essence of prayer: a heart-to-heart relationship; from

We find someone who can encourage, strengthen and challenge us to the roots, someone who can draw out of us what we hardly realized we had it in us to be.

the heart of God to humankind, from the heart of humankind to God—and with complete honesty on both sides.

In exploring such prayer, the Passion of Jesus is a good place to begin, for there the matter is focused most sharply and starkly. So let us look at the night before Christ's death.

'In the same night that he was betrayed,' as the eucharistic prayer so tellingly puts it, Jesus engaged in much prayer. He was facing the greatest crisis of his life. Prayer was his primary and fundamental response. Such had evidently been the case in a variety of situations during his public ministry. It had no doubt also characterized his life in that long hidden period before his baptism in the Jordan. For Jesus, prayer was inseparable from life and work. Prayer was his life-breath. Prayer permeated his being. For prayer was nothing less than living life, with and in God.

In the same night that he was betrayed, 'Jesus took bread, and

For Jesus, prayer was inseparable from life and work. Prayer was his life-breath. Prayer permeated his being. For prayer was nothing less than living life, with and in God.

blessed and broke it, and gave it to the disciples and said, "Take, eat; this is my body". And he took a cup, and when he had given thanks he gave it to them, saying, "Drink of it, all of you; for this is my blood of the covenant, which is poured out for many for the forgiveness of sins"' (Matthew 26:26–28).

They were all sitting at supper, Jesus and the Twelve (and possibly others). It was a scene that must have been repeated many, many times before. Table fellowship was clearly important to Jesus. According to three of the Gospel writers (Matthew, Mark and Luke) this particular supper was a celebratory one, a meal to mark the feast of Passover.

On this occasion, however, Jesus was not just looking back to past bitter oppression from which his people had been delivered. He was looking forward to the bitterness of his own suffering, ultimate expression of the love and forgiveness of God, a new and greater Passover, the offering of a deeper relationship (or covenant) with God.

He gave thanks over bread and wine; a familiar practice, but surely, for Jesus. far more than a mechanical saying of grace. Jesus delighted in the good things of God's creation and saw the presence and messages of God both in *them*, and in the mundane details of everyday life. To borrow George Herbert's phrase, Jesus saw and affirmed 'heaven in ordinarie'.

His teaching is full of it. The lilies of the field, a woman sweeping a room, a parent having problems with children—all these, and many more, are means of discerning the active involvement of God in the world. To Jesus, this was indeed something to rejoice in.

From the whole tenor of his ministry, and from the tantalizing glimpses we have into his prayer life, it seems that Jesus was given to rejoicing and exultation. He exults in the Holy Spirit. He gives thanks to God. He is full of vitality and *joie-de-vivre*. Tragically, it is the blinkered vision and fearful hardness of heart of the formal religious establishment that, in the end, hammers the joy out of him.

Even so, it burst out again 'with a vengeance' on Easter morning. Whatever the provocation, God and joy will not be finally separated. To the ages of ages, they belong together.

Bread and wine. Staple of life, and that which makes the heart glad. Reason enough to give thanks. But now, after this momentous supper, there is more. Now bread and wine become 'outward and visible signs' of the redeeming self-giving of God, that God from whom we derive both life and gladness.

As we eat and drink in faith, the reality to which the signs point nourishes our being. Our joy and pain are united with the pain and joy of God.

> *Jesus delighted in the good things of God's creation and saw the presence and messages of God, both in them, and in the mundane details of everyday life.*

Holiday Reading

Shelagh Brown

When he goes on holidays a vicar I know always takes lots of books with him to read. They fall into two clearly defined categories: secular books (detective stories and novels) and theological books. And he invariably reads the detective stories and novels first, and brings back the theological books almost invariably unopened. I used to do just the same—but as I have got a bit older I have become a bit wiser. Now I take just *one* religious book and really feed on it—so long as I'm feeling hungry for it.

For me that works—and I remember one year sitting on the beach at St Ives in Cornwall reading an old classic: *The Spirit of God* by Dr Campbell Morgan. I was exhilarated by it—and I could see the sheer efficiency and glory of God's plan of salvation (the Holy Spirit of God lives *in* us) far more clearly and understand it far more deeply. John Polkinghorne's *Science and the Providence of God* had the same exhilarating and enlarging effect when I was on my ordination retreat before being priested.

> *One of the most important things I learned ... was the truth that 'We can't do everything!'*

Recently I went on a course on managing priorities and meeting deadlines and one of the most important things I learned from it was the truth that 'We can't do everything!' I don't like having to believe it (and I'm having to work quite hard on doing so) because I feel that if only I worked harder and was more organized then I *would* be able to do everything. Or at least, everything I want to do. And that's true of reading as well as other things. It's all right to put everything down on our 'To Read List'—and make sure we have a selection of subjects. Some spiritual and theological books (not every one reviewed in *Theology* or *The Church of England Newspaper* or *Renewal*), some of the latest popular paperbacks, and a classic or two. But then we need to pull out the priorities and make a realistic and sensible choice: for most of us just *one* spiritual or theological book— and the rest of them for relaxation. That's what holidays are for, and we need them.

Holidays come from holy days, so *some* spiritual reading is good and necessary for our re-creation and refreshing, and our spirits need feeding and exercising just as our bodies do. St Ignatius knew what he was doing when he created The Spiritual Exercises, and in the hundreds of years since he wrote about them and explained how to use them thousands of people have discovered their enormous value.

This article is about holiday reading in general, not about BRF books in particular. You may well have one particular book in mind for your spiritual reading. If not, then I offer you a suggestion. One of Bill Sykes' *Visions* books would give you some rich and varied food for thought and meditation. Choose just one subject a day—and enjoy it.

> *We need to make a realistic choice... just one spiritual or theological book—and the rest of them for relaxation.*

The *Visions* series is available from your local Christian bookshop or, in case of difficulty, direct from BRF. See order form on page 159 for details.

The unregretfulness of God

John Fenton

It must, of course, be true that there is a vast difference between God as he is, and our ideas about him. If it were not so, he would not be God. We can only take in as much as we have the capacity for understanding, and, in the case of God, that must be less than the whole truth.

Nevertheless, it does not follow from this that it does not matter what we say about God, or what we think about him. There are still mistakes that can be made, or so those who believe in God will always maintain. He is not cruel or uncaring; he has no competitors; it is not true that he does not exist. One idea about God that seems to have gained popularity recently is that he is disappointed, heart-broken, in despair; that he regrets ever having made the world, and that he wishes he had never permitted the existence of human beings.

There is some support in scrip-

> *One idea about God that seems to have gained popularity recently is that he is disappointed, heart-broken, in despair.*

ture for thinking about God in this way. For example, in the introduction to the story of the flood:

'When the Lord saw how great was the wickedness of human beings on earth, and how their every thought and inclination were always wicked, he bitterly regretted that he had made mankind on earth.' (Genesis 6:5,6)

Though it should be noticed that the story ends with God's promise that he will never again put the earth under a curse because of mankind (8:21); the rainbow is the sign of this covenant (9:12–14). Another example of divine regretfulness in scripture is the appointment of Saul as king (1 Samuel 15:11, 35). In contrast with this is a group of passages in which it is said that God does not change his mind; for example, there is Balaam's question:

'God is not a mortal that he should lie, not a man that he should change his mind. Would he speak, and not make it good? What he proclaims, will he not fulfil?' (Numbers 23:19)

A notable instance of a biblical writer affirming the unregretfulness of God comes in Paul's letter to the Romans; the translation of it in the Revised English Bible is: 'The gracious gifts of God and his calling are irrevocable' (Romans 11:29).

More literally, with the word to be emphasized at the beginning of the sentence, it could be reordered:

'Not to be regretted are the free gifts and the calling of God'—meaning, God does not regret what he has done in giving his gifts to Israel and in calling them his people. (The only other place in the New Testament where the word here translated 'not to be regretted'

God is not to be thought of as one who has failed; he does not back losers; he is not incompetent; he has wisdom and knowledge incomparable

occurs is in 2 Corinthians 7:10, where Paul says that the Corinthians' previous pain caused by his letter to them will not be regretted, by him or by them.)

The argument in Romans 9 and 11 is that though the unbelief of the majority of Jews causes Paul great grief and unceasing sorrow in his heart (9:2), he still looks forward to the time when God's purpose will be worked out fully, in mercy to all mankind (11:2). God is not to be thought of as one who has failed; he does not back losers; he is not incompetent; he has wisdom and knowledge incomparable (11:33–36).

To think otherwise would be to make God in our image and to attribute to him the limitations under which we live. It is frequently a consequence of our ignorance that we act in ways that lead us to disappointment and regret: we are taken in by people, or we are blind to their faults, or we fail to take account of circumstances. None of this can apply to God. He knows what he is doing and he can foresee the consequences of it—so Paul believed; and it is hard to think otherwise of God. Even the consequences of human freedom need not be thought the cause of God's failure, as though it took him by surprise. 'Would he speak, and not make it good?', as Balaam asked; must we not think of him as fore-seeing and containing within his good purpose everything that would or could happen?

How did Paul come to be able to state so clearly the unregretful-ness of God? Possibly it was through reflect-ing on the crucifixion and resurrection of Jesus. On a purely human view, the death of Jesus looked like the failure of a mission: he had per-suaded no one to stand by him, according to Mark; his fol-lowers had run away, betrayed him and dis-owned him. But this was not the whole of the matter. Paul had at one time thought it was, but now he sees that it was not. 'The folly of God is wiser than human wisdom, and the weakness of God stronger than human strength' (1 Corinth-ians 1:25). What hap-pened was meant to happen.

Regret, sense of failure, disappoint-ment, unhappiness, should not be attrib-uted to God, but wis-dom, skill, knowl-edge, complete and inevitable eventual success; and above all, joy. We have become so used to responding to appeals for our sympathy, that we even suppose that we should be sorry for God. This is no way to think of the one who is the begin-ning and the end of all things, blessed for ever; nor is it any way to help people to believe in him. No one wants yet another person to be sorry for.

> *We have become so used to responding to appeals for our sympathy, that we even suppose that we should be sorry for God.*

John Fenton *is the author of* The Matthew Passion, *and of* Galatians *in the* People's Bible Commentary *Series. Both are published by BRF and are available from your local Christian bookshop or, in case of difficulty, direct from BRF. For details, see order form, page 159.*

The work of the Spirit

Our theme for the next two weeks is the work of the Holy Spirit, which is especially appropriate at the moment, not just because it is Pentecost, but because it is a subject of great concern, not to say confusion, to many contemporary Christians. We all need to evaluate for ourselves the experiences and claims of the charismatic renewal. Moreover, whatever our verdict about that may be, we cannot but be aware that the churches stand in great need of a new infusion of life and vitality that can only come from God through the action of his Spirit.

It will therefore be helpful for us to look at some scripture passages that open up for us what some of the biblical authors have to say about the work of the Holy Spirit. We shall start in the Old Testament with the prophet Ezekiel, whose writings are especially relevant to us because his situation has marked similarities to our own.

We shall then go on to passages in the Gospels that establish the most intimate connection between the work of the Spirit and the work of Jesus. We shall soon realize that, if we are to remain true to the New Testament, we cannot talk about the one without immediately referring to the other. Jesus is who he is and does what he does because he has received the Spirit from the Father and then gives the Spirit to us. The Spirit is the gift of the Father first *to* and then *through* the Son, so that his work is always to be seen in a trinitarian context.

Finally, we shall study some passages from the Pauline letters as he helps the young churches to understand and appropriate all that the Spirit has been doing among them since the Day of Pentecost. Our prayer and hope must be that through this study we shall come to a greater discernment about, and openness to, what the Spirit is doing and wants to do in the Church in our day.

Quotations throughout are from the New International Version of the Bible.

1 The valley of the bones   *Read Ezekiel 37:1–6*

The New Testament describes a people full of the power of the Spirit; this passage starts with a desolate people in desperate need of the new life that only the Spirit can bring. Ezekiel in his vision pictures the Israel of his day in terms of bodies so long dead on a defeated battlefield that they are reduced to a heap of dry bones. In the interpretation of the vision in the next part of the chapter we are told, 'These bones are the whole house of Israel. They say, "Our bones are dried up and our hope is gone; we are cut off"' (37:11). Those of us who have lived in a church that has been in institutional, and perhaps spiritual, decline for our whole lifetime have little difficulty in making the prophet's vision and his distress our own.

But Ezekiel, centuries before the first Easter, knows the God who loves graveyards and who can raise the question of resurrection precisely in the place and at the point where, by every human reckoning, such a thing has proved itself to be impossible. 'He asked me, "Son of man, can these bones live?"' (v. 3).

The prophet's response is highly instructive. 'I said, "O Sovereign Lord, you alone know."' The one who has raised the question must be the one who answers it. The resurrection of dry bones does not belong to the natural human agenda; no human effort or programme has any hope of bringing it about. Either God will do it or it will not be done at all. There are times in the Church's history when it can do nothing at all to rescue itself and its mission, when it is thrown back in utter dependence on the life-giving Spirit of its God.

It is precisely at these points of human helplessness that God takes over and comes good on his promises, 'I will put breath in you and you will come to life. Then you will know that I am the Lord' (v. 6). Only the Creator can recreate, only he who gave life at the beginning can give it again when it is gone. He who breathed the breath (= spirit) of life into Adam in Eden will breathe out the same breath/life on his desolate Israel, so that the dry bones become a mighty army by his Spirit and his grace.

2   The bones and the breath   *Read Ezekiel 37:7–14*

Having surveyed the desolate scene, the prophet in his vision becomes the human means through which God does his seemingly impossible work of resurrection. He receives two commands to prophesy, first to the bones and then to the breath.

First he is told to address the bones: 'Then he said to me, "Prophesy to these bones and say to them, 'Dry bones, hear the word of the Lord!' " ' (v. 4). If life is to return to God's people, they must first become attentive in a new way to God's word. When God's word is spoken and heard the dry bones are reorganized in a way that makes life possible again. For Christians this means that when the Church turns to God's word incarnate in Christ, written in scripture and interpreted in tradition, its life gains substance and strength from its gospel and it has the basic structure in place that will enable it to handle new life when it comes.

But lifeless skeletons with all the bones in place are not yet a living army. After Ezekiel has preached to the bones, he is told to pray for the breath (v. 9). The Hebrew word used here can equally well be translated as wind, breath or spirit. It speaks of the invisible, uncontrollable Spirit of God whose coming is needed to give the breath of new life to God's people. This is the Spirit which Jesus in John 3:8 compared to the wind which blows where it will. This Spirit cannot be controlled, but he is promised and in his own way and his own time he will come when he is prayed for.

The vision in verse 10 records the fact and the revolutionary effect of that coming and verse 14 interprets its meaning for Ezekiel's Israel and for us. This is God's promise by which the Church lives: 'I will put my Spirit in you and you will live.'

Word without breath cannot be spoken; breath without word is energy without significance. For its renewal the Church needs both the word of God to shape it and the Spirit of God to enliven it with his resurrection life.

3   The stream from the temple   *Read Ezekiel 47:1–6a*

Two of the main biblical metaphors for the Spirit are wind and water. In Ezekiel 37 the Spirit is the wind of God that gives breath to the dead; here in a fresh vision the Spirit is the living water that gives freshness and growth to what is withered and dry.

In Ezekiel's day Jerusalem was in ruins but in this vision he is shown the city rebuilt with the restored temple in its midst. From the altar which is the place of worship and sacrifice at the centre of the temple, a great river rises and runs out from the holy place into the streets of the city, making towards the east and deepening as it goes.

New life will come to the city from the place where people open themselves in worship to the living God and in sacrifice offer him themselves and their gifts. When that life comes, it cannot be contained within the world of religion where it starts; it is a river with its own direction and momentum and it makes its relentless way out from the realm of the sacred into the realm of the secular. It is a gift given through the temple but it is for the city and the wilderness beyond. God's Spirit is given not just to edify and uplift God's worshippers but to renew and refresh all God's people and indeed God's whole creation.

The prophet is made aware of the man with the measuring line who shows him how this river deepens as it goes. First it is ankle deep, then knee deep, then waist deep. To that point you can stand in it on your own feet and stay in control. But there comes a point where you get out of your depth and you have to swim, so that you trust yourself to the water and let it carry you.

It may be all right to start with paddling parties in God's living water, exposing only our extremities to its cleansing power, but the point will come when we have to surrender ourselves to the Spirit, let God's tides carry us in his chosen direction and trust ourselves to the deep currents of his purposes and his love.

4   The life-giving river   *Read Ezekiel 47:6b–12*

We have looked at the source and the course of God's river; now we see the direction it takes and the effects it achieves.

'He said to me, "This water flows towards the eastern region and goes down into the Arabah where it enters the Sea."' The Arabah is the eastern region of Judea which is so dry that little can grow in it; the Sea is the Dead Sea, so salty that nothing can live in it. In their direction God's river flows, to make the barren fertile and to turn the place of death into the place of life. The result is that along the banks of this river the trees whose roots are refreshed by its water become extraordinarily fruitful (v. 12) and the villages by the Dead Sea become the resorts of fishermen and good places to spread nets for a catch (vv. 9–10).

God's Spirit will always seek out our places of dryness and death. He is the Spirit of fruitfulness and new life. He is recognized not by bizarre manifestations but by the freshness and the creativity that breaks out among God's people as a result of his presence. 'Where the river flows everything will live' (v. 9).

The fruit of the Spirit is remarkable because it flourishes not only in favourable conditions or at special times of renewal but in the coldness of winter as well as in the warmth of summer. Ezekiel's trees are evergreen, their harvest appears in all seasons. God's fruit does not need specially heated conservatories to ripen; it is hardy enough for the ordinary and often adverse conditions of every day.

The New Testament commentary on this passage is in Revelation 22:1–2: 'Then the angel showed me the river of the water of life, as clear as crystal, flowing from the throne of God and of the Lamb, down the middle of the great street of the city. On each side of the river stood the tree of life, bearing twelve crops of fruit, yielding its fruit every month. And the leaves of the tree are for the healing of the nations.'

5 Spiritual anointing and social action   Read Isaiah 61:1–3; Luke 4:14–21

A comparison of these two passages provides our transition from Old Testament to New Testament teaching about the Holy Spirit. The same comparison emphasizes the continuity between the two, because the programme of the Old Testament prophet becomes the manifesto of the New Testament Messiah. For Jesus these words on the lips of the prophet are seen as promise awaiting future fulfilment; this they find only in himself and his ministry (Luke 4:21).

That ministry has had its beginning in the anointing of the Spirit. Here we encounter the third dominant biblical metaphor for the Spirit. Not only is he wind and water, but also the oil of anointing that inaugurates people into their callings as prophets, priests or kings. The word *Messiah*, in its Greek form *Christ*, means the anointed one. Jesus in his baptism is anointed by his Father with the Holy Spirit (Luke 3:21–22) for the ministry that he describes by quoting this Isaiah passage.

Personal anointing leads to liberating social action. Good news can be brought to the poor, freedom to the frustrated, sight to the blind, release to the oppressed only by someone who, like Jesus, is anointed by God's own Spirit. Conversely the sign that we have been filled by the Spirit that anointed Jesus is that we should make his manifesto our own and become involved in the liberation of others, which is the chief work of the Spirit. Without the Spirit, action on behalf of others will be in danger of running out of steam; without commitment to others, the energy of the Spirit will be in danger of being misused for our own enjoyment and self-fulfilment.

In quoting Isaiah 61 in the synagogue at Nazareth, there is one phrase which Jesus significantly omits. We hear of the 'year of the Lord's favour' but not of 'the day of vengeance of our God' (cf. Luke 4:19; Isaiah 61:3). The ministry of Jesus in the Spirit is unalloyed good news to all who will receive it. The threats and the condemnations remain unuttered; he comes not to impose them but, in his grace and by his cross, to bear them and take them away.

6   The Son and the Spirit   *Read John 1:29–34*

John's Gospel does not describe the baptism of Jesus but in this passage it interprets that event and, through the witness of John the Baptist, presents it to us as the conferring of the Holy Spirit upon the Son of God so that he may in turn confer him upon us.

First we are shown Jesus as 'the man on whom you see the Spirit come down and remain' (v. 33). Both verbs are significant. In his baptism, which is his commissioning as God's Son for his unique ministry, the Spirit comes down on Jesus. His coming in this way does not imply his absence from the life of Jesus up to that moment. This is a new coming, but not a first coming. According to Luke's story, the conception of Jesus in Mary's womb is already a great work of the Holy Spirit. Now however, when the years of privacy are over and the public ministry is about to start, the Spirit who came once to conceive comes again in a new way to empower. To have received him in one way in the past should make us ready to receive him in a new and different way in the future.

The Spirit who comes on Jesus *remains* on him. This is emphasized twice (vv. 32, 33). The Spirit of God takes up residence in the incarnate Son of God, who becomes the home base for all his operations in the world. He is like a dove who homes in on Jesus; fully to know the Spirit is to know that he comes from Jesus and leads back to Jesus. To deny his source and to refuse to move with him to his destination is to frustrate his work.

In the Spirit the Father gives himself to his Son and takes up his dwelling in him; in the Spirit the Son gives himself to us and takes up his dwelling in us. 'The man on whom you see the Spirit come down and remain is he who will baptise with the Holy Spirit' (v. 33). To seek the Spirit we must seek Jesus; he has the Spirit in such fulness that he is able to baptize us, that is, to plunge us into the depths of his life, love and power.

GUIDELINES

The sixty-four thousand dollar question that our readings so far raise for us is quite simply, Do we believe it? Is there a word of God that has power to shape and consolidate the Christian community? Is there a Spirit of God who can perform works of resurrection amidst contexts of ruin? Can God by that Spirit breathe new life on his people when they seem bound for death? Can he refresh them like water when they are dry and bitter? Can he anoint them with the energy to go out with good news to the impoverishment, frustration and blindness of the society around us? Are there still good grounds for the prophets' expectation that God must and can do these great things for us before we can begin to do anything much that matters for him?

These are questions that these passages encourage us to ask corporately about the people of God and their mission, and personally about ourselves and our part in the Church and its mission. The Holy Spirit is God in the present tense. When we are thinking about him, we cannot escape into past history or theoretical theology, but must ask ourselves whether we are believing enough, open enough, brave enough to pray, 'Holy Spirit, for a new day and in a new way come and do it all again for us now.'

12–18 MAY

1 By water and the Spirit *Read John 3:1–7*

If Nicodemus is to enter the realm in which the rule of God becomes visible and active in his life, he must be 'born of water and the Spirit'. Jesus, the king of the kingdom, entered it by the waters of his Jordan baptism and by the descent of his Father's Spirit upon him; if

Nicodemus is to enter the same kingdom he must do so in the same way. Religious activity, ecclesiastical position and moral rectitude are not by themselves passports into that kingdom; they belong to the realm of human achievement—'flesh' (v. 6). They are no substitute for that sovereign act, whereby in his own way and his own time the Spirit of God brings a person into a new relationship with God that can be called 'birth from above', because through it a new life begins.

In this passage the symbolic Old Testament connection between water and the Spirit that we saw in Ezekiel 47 is reaffirmed and applied to Christian baptism. Throughout John's Gospel Jesus often speaks of the Spirit in terms of water, more often water to drink rather than water to wash in, as though to emphasize the deep inner revitalization that the Spirit brings.

So, in the next chapter, Jesus speaks to the Samaritan woman of the water that he can give that will permanently quench our deepest thirsts by becoming in us 'a spring of water welling up to eternal life' (4:13–14). In chapter 7 at the Feast of Tabernacles 'Jesus stood and said in a loud voice, "If anyone is thirsty, let him come to me and drink. Whoever believes in me, as the Scripture has said, streams of living water will flow from within him"', to which the evangelist adds the comment, 'By this he meant the Spirit, whom those who believed in him were later to receive. Up to that time the Spirit had not been given, since Jesus had not yet been glorified' (7:37–39).

For John the place at which Jesus is glorified and the Spirit is given is the cross. It is from the side of the crucified Jesus, pierced by the Roman soldier's spear, that along with the blood which is the sign of redemption, the water which is the sign of the Spirit flows in free abundance to all who believe in him (19:34). The Spirit reaches us from the cross.

2 The coming Counsellor *Read John 16:5–11*

In the Farewell Discourses in John 14–16 we have some of the richest New Testament material about the work of the Holy Spirit and his relationship to Christ. It is probably based on an amalgam of the remembered teaching of Jesus and the actual experience of the apostles after his departure.

The distinctive title given to the Spirit here is in Greek *parakletos*, anglicized as Paraclete and variously translated as Comforter, Counsellor, Advocate. Its basic meaning is one called to the side of another to provide encouragement, help and strength. Its special context is the law courts, to describe the Advocate (or, in America, the Counsellor) who helps me by representing me and pleading my cause.

The commentators argue whether in these chapters the Holy Spirit is presented as the one who pleads our cause with God or alternatively as the one who pleads God's cause with us. We shall see later that the first meaning fits well with what Paul says about the Spirit in Romans 8, but here the main emphasis is on the Spirit who advocates Christ's cause in the forum of our minds and hearts.

The coming of the Spirit is dependent on the departure of Jesus (v. 7), so that there is a clear distinction between them. At the same time the coming of the Spirit is still in some sense the coming of Jesus, as 14:16–18 makes clear. The 'other Counsellor' whom Jesus sends is so closely identified with the Father and the Son, from and through whom he comes, that he can act as their divine representative and advocate among the disciple company.

Jesus goes on to enumerate different aspects of the Spirit's work. Verses 8–11 are not easy to understand in detail but the general point that they are making is quite clear. The Spirit is the one who illuminates our moral judgments by the light of the gospel, so that we can come to a discernment of what the God who is present in Christ judges to be right and wrong in the actions of his people and of the world in which they live. This is a discernment much to be sought in the perplexities of our own day.

3 The Spirit glorifies Jesus   Read John 16:12–15

In these verses Jesus goes on preparing his disciples for what the Spirit will begin to do among them after he himself has gone. The Spirit will relate what Jesus has done in the past to the new needs and situations in which the disciples are going to be involved in the future. He will show himself to be both the Spirit of faithfulness and the Spirit of relevance.

In all that he does the Spirit will prove himself to be faithful to Jesus. 'He will not speak on his own; he will speak only what he hears' (v. 13), and 'the Spirit will take from what is mine and make it known to you' (v. 15). To say that 'he will guide you into all truth' means that he will always guide us into the way of Jesus, who is himself the truth (14:6). Thus there will always be continuity between the gospel of the Son and the leading of the Spirit. New truth will always confirm and expand but never contradict old truth, when the Spirit is at work.

On the other hand it will never be enough simply to repeat the gospel; it needs to be interpreted and applied to new problems and new situations that could not have been encountered or even envisaged in the world where it was first declared. 'I have much more to say to you than you can now bear' (v. 12). It is the business of the Spirit to make what Jesus said as a first-century man to first-century people relevant to twenty-first-century people and the world in which they live. The Spirit glorifies Jesus by showing that his word is endlessly illuminating and creative down all the centuries and across all the continents.

The Church is often challenged by and in conflict with the different cultures within which it pursues its mission. This often results in perplexing internal controversies about what to believe and how to act. Our hope, founded on the promise of Jesus and the experience of our history, is that within these situations the Holy Spirit will, as Jesus promised, continue to lead us into a truth that is both faithful to his gospel and relevant to our times. Thus Jesus is glorified.

4 The Spirit in prayer   Read Romans 8:14–17, 26–34

God comes to us in order that we may then come to him. In this Pauline passage we see how the Spirit through Christ enables us to come to God in prayer.

Here we can see how Christian prayer is an implicitly trinitarian activity. Through Christ God reveals himself as our Father and through the Spirit we begin to regard ourselves as his children who can approach him with unbounded confidence. Because we are his children, we are also his heirs, indeed joint-heirs with Christ, so that everything he gave Jesus he is pledged to give us also, and to bring us through our sufferings to his glory. In the Spirit we can enter into that intimate relationship with the Father that Jesus enjoyed and that is expressed in the word *Abba*, Jesus' very characteristic name for God (vv. 14–17).

Prayer is of course a perplexing affair, as Paul confesses, so that it is easy for us to become discouraged by our inability to know how to pray and what to pray for (v. 26). However, our encouragement is that we are not left alone in our praying. There is one who prays *for* us and there is one who prays *in* us, and, however stumbling our praying may be, their prayer on our behalf ensures our access to the Father.

The ascended Christ is at the right hand of God and intercedes for us there (v. 34), and the prayer that he prays in heaven is echoed by the Spirit who prays the same prayer at the depths of our being at a level too deep for words to express (v. 26). This prayer of the Spirit is an intercession for all God's people and, whatever we may be asking on the surface level, he prays deep within us in a way that is in perfect accord with God's will and purpose for the situations and people who need his help (v. 27).

At the heart of all our praying and prior to all our speaking, there has to be a tuning in to the prayer of the Spirit that is already being prayed within us. This prayer is in union with the prayer of the ascended Christ on our behalf, and brings us into the presence and love of the Father from whom they both come and to whom they bring us home.

5 The Spirit of resurrection   *Read Ephesians 1:13–23*

Here we move from Pauline teaching about the Spirit's part in our praying to an actual example of a Pauline prayer for the Spirit. So verse 17: 'I keep asking that the God of our Lord Jesus Christ, the glorious Father, may give you the Spirit of wisdom and revelation, so that you may know him better.' We should note the following points.

First this is a *trinitarian* prayer. He approaches the Father who is accessible in the Son and asks him for the gift of the Spirit.

Secondly, this is a *corporate* prayer. The 'you' for whom he seeks the Spirit is the corporate body of the Ephesian church rather than its individual members. We need to pray for churches, that the Spirit who indwells their fellowship and shapes their members should be the Holy Spirit and not one of these very unholy spirits that can hold Christian congregations in thrall.

Thirdly, to pray for a fresh gift of the Spirit does not imply that he is not already present and at work. Paul says that he 'keeps on asking' that the Spirit who has already been at work at Ephesus may go on working in new ways, in new people and new situations, so that they 'may know him better'. One of the signs that we are already in the Spirit is that we should continually pray for more of the Spirit.

Here he does not pray for particular gifts of the Spirit such as tongues, prophecy and healing, but rather for an increase in knowledge of God, of hope for the future and the release of resurrection power among God's people (v. 18).

The Spirit who works in Ephesus is the same Spirit who was at work in the tomb of Jesus on Easter morning (v. 20). For us, as for Jesus, the fulness of resurrection lies on the other side of physical death, but there are signs and promises of resurrection life that break out in churches and people here and now. In verse 13 Paul speaks of the Holy Spirit as the 'deposit' or better 'first instalment that guarantees all that is still to come'. We are to ask him to do among us now things that will point to the great resurrection still to come.

6 The Spirit of Pentecost   *Read Acts 2:1–47*

This is of course the passage that everyone associates with the gift of the Holy Spirit. We have left it to the end so that we may see it in the whole rich context of the biblical teaching about the Spirit of which our passages have reminded us. What happened at Pentecost was not just a dramatic event with remarkable phenomena attached to it. It was nothing less than the beginning of the fulfilment of the Old Testament promises of the Spirit, as Peter points out in relation to Joel (v. 16), and the conveying to the disciples of the personal divine presence and power that had guided and activated Jesus and was now to guide and activate them.

The reference back to Jesus becomes explicit in verse 33: 'Exalted to the right hand of God, he has received from the Father the promised Holy Spirit and has poured out what you now see and hear.' The Holy Spirit comes from God via Jesus and he bears upon him the marks of his origin. He comes not to create sensations, but to reproduce in us the character and the ability of the Lord Jesus Christ. He does this, however, not only in the secret places of our hearts, but in the public world where the results of his activity can be seen and heard, as they were on the day of Pentecost.

He works not just in the realm of inward experience but in the world of outward eventfulness, as this chapter demonstrates. The fearful disciples are confident enough to declare themselves before a potentially crucifying Jerusalem public. The gospel becomes accessible to people of different languages and cultures (v. 11). Peter's preaching is powerful enough to convert three thousand people (v. 41). The disciple company becomes open to God in a new way and overflows with a generous love that expresses itself in a very practical and down-to-earth sharing of resources (vv. 42–47).

All these are outward and visible signs of a church that has been baptized, i.e. flooded, with the Holy Spirit. Such a church becomes fascinating and attractive to people who before have been indifferent or hostile towards it. It is to a such a church, then and now, that the Lord adds 'those who were being saved' (v. 47).

GUIDELINES

In relation to the passages we have been studying, we have often had reason to speak of the *gift* of the Holy Spirit—not just of the various gifts that he can give us, but of the Spirit himself as God's gift of himself to us.

We cannot do better than end by taking to ourselves the words of Jesus in Luke 11:13, in which he offers that gift to us and assures us that, because of the glorious generosity of his Father, it will he ours for the asking. 'If you then, though you are evil, know how to go on giving good gifts to your children, how much more will your Father in heaven go on giving the Holy Spirit to those who go on asking him.'

Such a translation makes it clear, in a way that is congenial to the whole context of the passage from which the verse comes, that the seeking and the receiving of the Spirit is a continuous rather than a once for all activity. We certainly need to seek the Spirit in the dire days of personal or corporate crisis, but we need to seek him also in the midst of the ordinary routines of life.

There will be nothing stereotyped or repetitive about the way he comes. He is the Spirit of endless creativity, who does the same work in a countless number of different ways. But always he will refresh our relationship to God, renew our fellowship with one another and take us one step further along the road of our transformation into the likeness of Christ.

Other spirits intrude and dominate where they are not wanted. The Holy Spirit comes only when he is sought and invited. He is given to those who ask for him. That seeking will take us deep into God and deep into ourselves, but it takes only a few words to express it: 'Come, Creator Spirit, to your world, to your church and to me.'

Deuteronomy

The book of Deuteronomy represents a 'second-giving' of the law of Moses which had already been revealed at Mount Sinai and is now recorded in the books of Exodus and Leviticus. The occasion for this repetition is the fact that Israel had by this time spent forty years in the wilderness (so Deuteronomy 1:3) and was about to embark upon the crossing of the river Jordan and the conquest and settlement of the land promised to its ancestors Abraham, Isaac and Jacob (Deuteronomy 1:8). However the book is clearly not a straightforward repetition of laws that had already been made known earlier, but represents both a summary of them, together with the addition of revisions and new rulings.

The primary setting for the book is that of a speech given by Moses on the eve of the crossing of the Jordan (Deuteronomy 4:21–24; 34:1–12). Alongside the laws themselves there are warnings and exhortations to the people to be prepared for the dangers and temptations that lie ahead. Nor were they to forget the mistakes and failings of the more recent past which had occasioned serious frustration and had come close to bringing complete catastrophe for the emergent nation of Israel. Such warnings are set out in a passionate preaching style which gives to the book its special character. It is the most often quoted Old Testament writing in the New, and its many warnings and threats make it a powerful and heart-searching uncovering of human nature, with all its hopes and weaknesses. Alongside this rich vein of spiritual perceptiveness there also lies a fierce and ruthless demand for religious purity, calling for the destruction of all physical artefacts of earlier religious life in the land and the extermination of its previous occupants without pity. In this respect the book falls far below even the minimum standard of Christian love and tolerance.

Although the heart of the book is a carefully compiled series of laws governing court rulings and procedures (chapters 12–26), much of this central part also deals with religious obligations and observances which were not narrowly legal. There is an important introduction to these laws in chapters 1–11, containing lengthy speeches from Moses which offer penetrating analyses of human selfishness and the human capacity for self-deception. They also provide deeply reflective and perceptive descriptions of God, relating the divine reality to the true nature of faith and worship, and showing how the roots of human sin are to be found in the false reasonings of the mind. The readings are taken from the New International Version.

19–25 MAY   **DEUTERONOMY 1–11**

1   **A time to move forward**   *Read Deuteronomy 1:1–33*

In spite of the primary setting of the book on the eve of Israel's crossing of the river Jordan in order to conquer the promised land, it becomes clear that the author recognizes that no less than three distinct generations of the Israelite people faced essentially the same crisis. This was a crisis of faith and obedience. The first such generation was that which stood at the foot of Mount Sinai (consistently called Horeb in Deuteronomy), and it is this which is reviewed here in chapter 1. The second such generation, faced with a similar crisis of faith, is that to whom the book as a whole is explicitly addressed in chapters 31–34. This generation was on the verge of crossing the river Jordan to conquer the land with strict instructions to make it pure from false (Canaanite) religion.

However there is a third generation of Israelites whose plight is less openly revealed in the book, but is undoubtedly present to the observant reader (especially in chapters 28–29). This third generation, who also faced a crisis of faith, was that which stood closest to the readers of the book in its finished form. They were a later generation who had settled in the land, but who had witnessed the loss of most of the territory which had once belonged to Israel. They now feared that they would lose it all and themselves be returned to slavery in Egypt (so Deuteromony 28:68). These three widely separated generations are recognized as sharing a common fundamental need to renew faith and commitment to the Lord as God. Accordingly the author pays great attention to past failures and acts of disloyalty, seeing in them signs of the deceitful nature of sin and offering painful lessons from which much could be learned of relevance to later generations.

So the warning concerning the first generation who had stood with Moses at Mount Horeb was a deeply meaningful one. That generation had wasted forty years in the wilderness (Deuteronomy 1:3) and forfeited their right to the land, because they had been fearful when they heard the report of the spies they had sent out (vv. 19–33). Only a few like Joshua had believed that God could give them victory. So only now, thirty-eight years later (Deuteronomy 2:14), had a new generation come into being to whom was given the command: 'Go in and take possession of the land' (v. 8). It was a message which had a continued and much needed relevance because it was a call for the renewal of faith.

Since it was essential that future generations should learn to live without Moses, who had himself been unable to enter the land, they would be able to make up for this by appointing authorized legal officials who would deal with disputes when they arose (vv. 9–18).

2 Be careful, and watch yourselves closely
Read Deuteronomy 4:1–31

Israel had survived the rigours and temptations of life in the wilderness under the leadership of Moses. It is the favourite theme of the author that there was no other leader of comparable greatness to him, and that without his wisdom and prayers the people would have perished quickly without ever seeing the promised land. Yet living without Moses was exactly what the people addressed by the author would have to do, so it was necessary that they should be warned of this necessity. The book of Deuteronomy itself is the first consequence of this, for it is the book of the laws that Moses gave, making it in a real sense a carrying forward of the work of Moses for the benefit of all future generations. In one sense Israel would never need to be without Moses, since they would always have the book of the laws through which his insights and understanding of truth had been granted to them. They were Israel's national treasure par excellence. The point is forcefully presented in verses 5–8. Moses' leadership remained a permanent gift to Israel.

However, it was evident that all kinds of hindrances and temptations would arise which might make the truth that Moses had given hard to find, or seemingly of little importance. The most dangerous of these was that presented by other forms of religion in which the mystery and hidden majestic power of God would be denied. In particular such pagan religion made use of an abundance of images and symbolism which could prove remarkably impressive.

So we are given a closely reasoned account of how God had been revealed on Mount Horeb, hidden by fire and black clouds, but without the actual form of God being seen (vv. 9–14). In place of images and idols, Israel instead enjoyed a knowledge of God through the law of Moses, which was far superior (v. 14). Idolatry was therefore irrelevant and forbidden (vv. 15–31).

3 The Ten Commandments   *Read Deuteronomy 5:1–21*

No part of the Old Testament has had greater influence upon Christianity, and upon human history more generally, than have the Ten Commandments set out here. Their repetition in Deuteronomy lends added emphasis to them, since they are first set out in Exodus 20:2–17. In one sense they stand apart from, and above, the other laws which form the revelation of God given through Moses. Yet, in another sense, they are a fundamental summary of the laws contained in the Old Testament as a whole, focusing on specific demands and attitudes. They are therefore less laws for a legislator to enact than declarations of principle, and have justifiably been compared to modern ideas of human rights. They affirm the necessity for recognizing that a commitment of faith to a divine supernatural Creator is essential if there is to be respect for the order and structure of the created world. So the commands calling for respect for God (vv. 6–15) take precedence over the commands for respect of the created order of life and society (vv. 16–21), with a clear recognition of their inter-relatedness.

Two are set out as positive commands ('Observe the sabbath day...', v. 12 and 'Honour your father and your mother...', v.16), whereas the others are prohibitions, excluding actions which infringe the divine order of life. The formal distinction is governed by the particular subjects dealt with. It is evident that the commandments aim to bring as wide as possible an area of basic conduct under a necessarily brief list of words which could easily be memorized, and even associated with the ten fingers of human hands. Their very brevity and directness has helped to make them one of the greatest guides to the fundamental nature of how human beings can live together in one world.

4 Love the Lord your God *Read Deuteronomy 6:1–25*

The Ten Commandments present a kind of map, or chart, setting out the basic rules for a God-planned quality of life between persons. There must be trust between people, respect for the sanctity of human life, loyalty within the family and protection for its children and aged members. Similarly there must be respect for truth and justice, to which all have fair and equal access. Yet these are principles of conduct which individual persons may themselves reject by rejecting the idea that God has any right to impose such demands upon human beings. They may argue that to adopt such a way of life is merely a matter of choice. So here in Deuteronomy 6 we have a series of admonitions which have become almost as well-known and important as the Ten Commandments themselves. They show the basic attitude and habit of mind that is needed for the way of life shown in the Commandments to be realized.

Two basic rules are set out which remain as powerful today as when they were first given. First is the demand that there must be a genuine love for God (v. 5). Nowhere else is the remarkable strength of Deuteronomy's understanding of faith better displayed than here. Setting aside self-interest and mere unwilling conformity, it urges a love for God which embraces all the strength and resources of human personality (v. 5). At the same time the commandments are to be taught earnestly at all times and to be recalled and remembered in all situations (vv. 6–9). Love for God can properly be commanded because its reasonableness and rightness can be taught. Nowhere else in the entire Bible is the connection between reasoned faith and education more firmly asserted than here! At the same time the comprehensiveness with which the entire make-up of the human personality is given one clear, simple and direct central focus is astounding. Being a whole integrated person requires a proper focus on God! How much of the stress and frustration of modern life results from neglect of this admonition and the consequent lack of any such focus?

5 Not by bread alone *Read Deuteronomy 8:1–20*

Much of the richness and enduring value of the teaching of Deuteronomy lies in its remarkable ability to penetrate beneath the exterior of human activity to probe the way in which people think and react to situations. So it can draw far-reaching lessons from the historical traditions of the past, which here concern the story of Israel's existence during forty years spent wandering in the wilderness. It was a time of harsh conditions and daily uncertainty, contrasting strongly with the rich plenty of life in the promised land (vv. 7–9). Yet in the time of uncertainty and danger God always provided enough to support the people, disciplining them, but not indulging them (vv. 5, 15–16). At that time the sense of dependence on God was everywhere paramount.

It is a paradoxical contrast that it is when there is abundance of everything that men and women forget God, even arrogantly presuming that they have achieved their success and prosperity by their own energies (v. 17). Temptation therefore comes, not from going without, which can be a good discipline as the Christian tradition of periodic fasting has sought to affirm, but from feeling self-satisfied and having no need of God. Is there a lesson here for the so-called 'First-World' nations to remember when thinking of the Third World? So often being materially rich leads to becoming spiritually impoverished. No wonder the message of Deuteronomy 8:3 became such a key text for Jesus when facing temptation in his own wilderness experience (Matthew 4:4).

6 The man God listened to · Read Deuteronomy 9:1–21

Nowhere is the praise of Moses as a faithful servant of God more highly celebrated than here, and the focus of this praise is to be found in verse 19: 'But again the Lord listened to me'! Moses was the man who saw things as they really were and who used that knowledge to take responsibility for the people. Accordingly, when he prayed, God listened! Once again we are presented with those key features of Deuteronomy which have made it such a rich mine of spiritual insight. The past is full of lessons because history is a pilgrimage which human beings conduct before God. But human nature is woefully fickle and prone to self-delusion. Even possessing such a rich and fruitful land as that given to Israel could make people feel good about themselves instead of thankful to God (vv. 4–6).

Similarly the giving of the law on Mount Horeb had been the greatest treasure for the future nation since it made possible a new, God-planned, order of life. But in the very moment when the people should have been rejoicing in this great gift, they were betraying their own recent experience and their own better selves, by making an idol in the shape of a calf (v. 16). The account is remarkable in its ability to uncover the fickleness and unreasoning nature of human faith and loyalty. Even in our best moments we shall not be wholly free from temptation and that temptation may well take the form of reducing God to something simple that we can manage. The repeated and passionate rejection of idolatry in Deuteronomy reflects its hatred of all forms of religion that are merely human constructions—powers which we believe we can make serve us, as the calf symbolized the power of fertility, and was believed to promote the productivity of flocks and herds. Such images promise divine power without demanding the way of life embodied in God's commandments. The temptation to look for a religion that has no commandments but merely offers supernatural power instead, has been a persistent human illusion. It is no wonder that Moses was so angry!

GUIDELINES

Two things are especially striking in looking back over the readings chosen from Deuteronomy 1–11. The first lies in the remarkable ability of the biblical author to unmask our innermost selves and to show up the kind of reasoning which we can be guilty of, but are never likely to admit. The most striking comes with the thought 'The Lord has brought me here... because of my righteousness' (9:4). We feel good about ourselves and our devotion to God may even add to this complacency. This was the mistake made by the well-intentioned Pharisee (in Luke 18:11–12). In a deep sense our very devotion can hide from us what a long way we still have to go to achieve the fulness of life made possible by God's commandments.

In a similar fashion our hard-working and responsible attitude to life may tempt us into feeling that 'My power and the strength of my hands have produced this wealth for me' (8:17). We then forget how much we owe to God and how deeply our very health, strength and skills are dependent on the grace of God shown to us through parents, friends and our settled circumstances of life. Would we enjoy as much had we been born in more straightened circumstances? So often it is seeing the grim shadow of poverty and hunger that hangs over others that reminds us of our ultimate dependence upon God.

More strikingly still all these speeches from Moses remind us how closely intertwined are the material and spiritual realms. It is how we conduct ourselves in relation to the possessions we have which provides the true barometer of our spiritual wealth. In the last resort the great error of idolatry lies in judging ourselves by what we have, rather than what we are as persons (compare Paul's comment concerning 'greed, which is idolatry' in Colossians 3:5). We still need Moses to set us right!

---

26 MAY–1 JUNE   **DEUTERONOMY 12–26**

1 **In the presence of the Lord your God**
   Read Deuteronomy 12:1–19

The heart of the book of Deuteronomy consists of a collection of laws which commence in chapter 12 with comprehensive regulations about God's sanctuary and conclude in chapter 26 with rules regarding the offering of tithes and firstfruits. Rules of life, governing legal, social and domestic affairs are set within a framework of worship. That is the way that Deuteronomy envisages the ideal society to be built. Faith provides a platform for shaping and regulating more secular activities. Whereas many of the laws proper show important links with similar laws from other ancient civilizations, those which govern worship are distinctively Israelite in character.

The opening provision in chapter 12 concerns the setting aside of a special place for worship where an altar was to be built and to which offerings would be made. To make such gifts at any other sanctuary, or to any other deity, was expressly forbidden under pain of the most serious penalties (chapter 13). In such fashion Israel's faith was to be kept pure. Throughout most of the period of biblical history this place of worship was undoubtedly that of Jerusalem.

Throughout Christian history we can see that demands for good order in worship have had to be tempered by the need for freedom to celebrate before God in genuinely personal and meaningful ways. So the firmness of the Deuteronomic rule to prevent worship 'according to our own desires' (v. 8) has to be seen in its context. All too easily well-intentioned freedom of expression can mean losing sight of the true majesty of God.

2 Open your hand to the poor   *Read Deuteronomy 15:1–18*

Just as the book of Deuteronomy recognizes that prosperity can give rise to a feeling of complacency, so also is it very conscious that money and wealth generally pose problems which have a deep spiritual connection. The society that is envisaged here was one in which the possession of wealth and its use to buy property and invest in merchant enterprises was an increasingly important aspect of life. In this regard it was a surprisingly 'modern' world. But money brought power and influence, leaving behind those who had been less successful in acquiring it and relegating them to poor health, limited opportunities and making them vulnerable to exploitation. Accordingly three regulations are here set out in order to alleviate these consequences. A year of remission of debts is proposed for every seventh year (vv. 1–6); to implement this a generous and ungrudging attitude towards the poor is called for (vv. 7–11). This is beautifully expressed in the words of the divine command 'Open your hand to the poor and needy neighbour in your land' (v. 11). Thirdly, even the slave, whether man or woman, was to be released after the completion of six years of slavery (vv. 12–15) unless they specifically requested to remain in their servitude (vv. 16–17). We must bear in mind that most slavery in ancient Israel occurred as a result of falling into debt so that recommencing life as a free citizen without capital was a daunting prospect (note the admonition of verse 13).

The particular rules set out in these laws now appear antiquated and of limited value in addressing the major problems of human poverty. It appears that even the ancient lawmakers recognized this fact, judging by the many exhortations that are added. Accordingly the major emphasis throughout these rules lies in their concern for a right attitude of mind, calling for liberality and an ungrudging willingness to give to those in need (v. 10). Even Israel's own cruel and impoverished origins needed to be remembered (v. 15). So well does the Bible uncover the innate tendency to selfishness in human life!

3 When things go wrong   *Read Deuteronomy 17:2–20*

Much that is most memorable in the book of Deuteronomy is to be found in its insights into human thinking and feeling. It recognizes that any call for spiritual wholeness is a very personal call which challenges our attitudes of mind. We have seen that even the problems caused by poverty are chiefly countered by appeals for a caring and unselfish attitude on the part of better off individuals. Yet society is more than a cluster of isolated individuals. Accordingly it must establish effective government of trusted and reliable men and women who will bear responsibility for just laws (vv. 2–7), and it must possess respected religious leaders who will mediate in serious disputes and feuds (vv. 8–13). At the head of the entire nation there should be a kingship in which the ruler is himself God-fearing and law-abiding (vv. 14–20).

Several features of what is called for in these laws are of special interest. It is taken for granted that, even in the best-regulated society, the actions of criminals and other wrongdoers must be reckoned with (v. 2). So an effective administration of law is essential. Yet, in order to be truly fair and just, the duty of the law is not only to punish offenders, but also to protect the innocent (hence the provisions of verses 6–7 in the case of capital charges). In their zeal to stop criminal actions, judges, and people generally, can all too readily be overbalanced in believing every charge of wrongdoing. Inevitably many cases would prove to be too difficult for achieving a convincing verdict. They would then fall outside the competence of the law officials to deal with. In these instances the matter was to be referred to the levitical priests who carried responsibility as mediators and guides in judging between feuding families and contested claims. When the law appeared ineffective avenging families could take action prematurely (which is why the 'cities of refuge' of Deuteronomy 19:1–13 were established). The experience and reputation for fairness of the priest was to be accepted without question (v. 12).

At the head of the nation would be the king, yet even he was a fallible human being who needed to study the law of God (vv. 18–19). Special emphasis is placed upon the insight that he should not regard himself to be above the rest of the community (v. 20), nor use his royal position as a means for grasping great wealth or making excessive displays of power (v. 17). He must never forget that he also is God's servant who would one day give account of his stewardship.

4 Faithful ministers and their counterfeits
Read Deuteronomy 18:1–22

The previous regulations have introduced us to three major professions of ancient Israel—lawyers, priests and the king, who would have been surrounded by a host of princes and court officials. Among these the profession of the priests was a particularly difficult and influential one, since the land to be occupied had a host of sanctuaries with their own local priestly servants. In addition alongside them were many freelance religious teachers and practitioners who claimed to give oracles, to heal diseases, to guarantee safe childbirth and to perform a host of personal ministries which might even extend to summoning the spirits of the dead to advise the living. Faithful priests and prophets, who were trustworthy, reliable and true to the teaching and spirit of Moses, were alone to be accepted and listened to. It was necessary therefore that they should be properly supported since their role in keeping the people faithful to God was paramount (vv. 1–8). If they were not adequately maintained then, inevitably, men and women would be tempted to resort to the age-old practitioners of pagan religion that abounded.

This introduces us to the fact that there existed considerable numbers of spurious, but plausible-sounding, religious tricksters. Their activities are listed in verse 10. Alongside the inevitable fortune-telling and divinatory practices we read of the particularly horrifying practice of the infanticide of unwanted daughters, as well as claims to consult with the dead. As so often in human history worthy and caring forms of faith and devotion could be counterfeited by false claimants, whose credentials were non-existent, but whose ability to prey on human fears and uncertainties made a living for them. All too often the corruption of what was good and honourable in religion could deceive the unwary. Even the passionate and earnest preaching of prophets could be simulated and counterfeited and needed to be guarded against (vv. 15–22).

5 You may not withhold your help *Read Deuteronomy 22:1–12*

We have noted how important it was for Deuteronomy to address individuals and to urge the adoption of right attitudes, beginning with love for God, but extending to recognize the needs and rights of neighbours. All too often the concept of a list of laws, setting out what must not be done, appears negative and limited in its value. Yet this is not the fundamental purpose of law, which is to uphold a just order for a caring society, with due respect for human freedom. A number of features of the regulations and laws set out here are of significance precisely because they presume that the duty of a good citizen includes accepting responsibility for others and providing assistance when encountering a problem situation. The rules of verses 1–4 provide important illustrations of principle. If a neighbour's beast was lost or in trouble, it was a duty to return it to its owner. You could not simply turn a blind eye, especially if you hoped to gain by doing so when it had strayed on your property!

The same sense of social responsibility is present in the laws of verses 6–12. The principles that undergird them presume that there is an order to the world which must be respected, so there is to be a rejection of the practices of wearing clothes appropriate to the opposite sex, the mixing of different kinds of seed in a single field, or yoking together different working beasts (v. 10). The law which commands the wearing of tassels on a cloak (v. 12) lacks any very obvious fundamental explanation as to its origin. In Numbers 15:37–41 the tassels attached to the edge of a garment were taken as reminders of the need for obedience to God's law in all things. Daily life took on a special meaning when it was seen to provide an opportunity for showing love and obedience to God.

6 You shall rejoice in all the good things
Read Deuteronomy 26:1–19

This section brings to a close the main legal and regulatory section of Deuteronomy. What follows takes the form of long speeches and addresses. It is appropriate therefore that the laws should close as they began with instructions for worship. All law is aimed at upholding the divine order of life in society. If its rules are kept, then the divine promise of prosperity and well-being can be fulfilled and its benefits enjoyed. Life would be good for Israel. Yet we have seen that behind the laws there is recognition of a deeper need for loyalty to God as the divine ruler of Israel. Unless that loyalty were maintained then the laws themselves would quickly be neglected and disregarded.

It is in response to this need that the section in verses 5–9 provides a short summary account of Israel's origins as a company of slaves in Egypt, rescued under the leadership of Moses and brought securely into the land promised to their ancestors. It is a history lesson, but not like any other history lesson simply recording past events, for it is a confession of faith, looking beyond the story of what had actually happened to the God who had led Israel to their land. It is not at all flattering to the people themselves, showing them to be helpless slaves who would have had nothing at all to bring to God, had it not been for God's prior gift of life and land. It is an object lesson in the way national history should be remembered—not as a call to unwarranted pride and sense of achievement, but as a story of grace and of God's unmerited goodness.

GUIDELINES

Through the New Testament letters of St. Paul we have learned to think of the laws of the Old Testament as severe and threatening. They demand from us a pattern of conduct and an integrity of purpose from which we all too readily fall short. However much we want to do the right thing towards our neighbours and fellow citizens we are conscious that we are far from being steadfast and consistent. The law seems always to mark us down when we err! Yet much of the importance of what Deuteronomy teaches about God's law is to be found in its emphasis upon the grace of God that exists behind and beyond the law. Law and grace are to be found in both Old and New Testaments for they are related aspects of the way in which God comes to us. The gracious call and redemption of God meets us before the law, as Israel's escape from Egypt took place before the law was given on Mount Sinai. Yet the life of salvation is not to be a law-less life, but one in which learning to respond to the love of God is displayed in loving one's neighbour. It is the grace of God that makes it possible for us to accept responsibility for ourselves, and our society and to fulfil the divine plan for human beings made in his image. Law shows us our need of grace and forgiveness, but in turn it is grace that shows us our need of God's law.

2–8 JUNE   DEUTERONOMY 27–34

1   God who sees in secret   *Read Deuteronomy 27:11–26*

We have already seen that the lists of laws in Deuteronomy seek to establish a proper and just way of life and to ensure complete loyalty to the Lord God of Israel. In order to achieve this the book demands harsh and cruel punishment for any citizens who betray their loyalty to God. At the same time it looks to the appointment of officials—

judges and priests—to administer the law. Yet they, and even the king at the head, were merely human beings who could only fulfil their duties with the skills and resources they possessed. Many crimes would inevitably be left undetected and unpunished and many wrongs could be carried out privately without ever being discovered.

The list of twelve curses in verses 15–26 are noteworthy because they show that, even with the best laws and the best judges, there were offences which were recognized to be beyond the power of human laws to deal with because they were never likely to be found out. Forbidden forms of idolatry and false religion could be carried on privately and secretly (v. 15). Anger, hate and cheating could be carried on within a home and not even a neighbour would know (vv. 16). So also many forbidden and unsuspected acts of sexual abuse could take place within the secrecy of a house, since people would believe the householder, rather than the victim. In some circumstances even murder itself could be perpetrated and the criminal never found out or apprehended (vv. 20–24). In fact, when opportunity permitted, many ways could be found for seeking to flout and cheat the law of God (vv. 19 and 25). Yet the law of God would not be cheated with impunity because God sees in secret and knows the thoughts of human hearts. The law itself was more than a set of rules where sometimes the wrongdoer might go undetected. Sooner or latter all must give account to God. By responding to the public listing of such offences with the word 'Amen', every citizen was placed under the strictest honour to fulfil the law of God. Even when fellow citizens were unsuspecting, God would not be!

2   The things revealed belong to us   *Read Deuteronomy 29:1–29*

Of all the many comments concerning the Old Testament law that provoke deep reflection that of St Paul in Romans 7:21: 'When I want to do good, evil is right there with me'—has proved to be both the most persistent and the most enigmatic. God's law shows us the right and intended path of goodness for which all human beings were created. Why then do we not obey it, and even appear to be incapable of doing so? St Paul's reflection is not unique to himself, nor to the New Testament alone, but finds a profound anticipation here in Deuteronomy. The passage draws together the experience of many generations of Israelites. First that generation which had stood at the foot of Mount Horeb and had actually witnessed the marvellous deliverance from the Egyptian pharaoh (v. 3); secondly those who were about to cross the River Jordan after forty years of wandering in the wilderness—they too had experienced the wonderful care of God's providence (vv. 5–8). Yet there would also be other later generations of Israelites who would become aware that their life in the land had failed to fulfil all their original expectations. Their very hold on the promised land would come under repeated threat.

There was a truth to be learned about human nature, closely in line with the later words of St Paul, that human minds and hearts are repeatedly guilty of an unwillingness to trust in God. There is a warp in the fabric of human minds and wills. Evidence for such disobedience is described powerfully in verses 18–28 in warnings of terrible destruction besetting Israel. Men and women would be asking 'Why has the Lord done this to the land?' (v. 24). The story of divine promise and power was repeatedly marred by experiences of inexplicable catastrophe. In this powerful speech Moses squarely points out where the blame lies: 'But to this day the Lord has not given you a mind that understands or eyes that see...' (v. 4).

In one clear challenge the fault is shown to lie deep down in human hearts. We so readily become the enemies of God, and in doing so become enemies to our own better selves. The mystery of sin blurs our vision and prevents us from seeing clearly where our own true interest lies.

3   Not beyond your reach   *Read Deuteronomy 30:1–20*

In recording the law given through Moses to Israel, the book of Deuteronomy summarizes the story of how the first founders of the nation experienced God's providential care in the wilderness. It sees that vital spiritual lessons for all generations of Israel were to be learned from their experience. Deep-rooted tendencies of human thought and attitude were brought to light which remained the same throughout later generations. The triumphant stories of courage and faith had constantly to be seen as mixed with parallel and related stories of human timidity and disobedience. The clarion call to loyalty that had been given to the first pioneers had even then, when men and women had actually witnessed the saving power of God, been followed by fear and unbelief.

The memory of such contrasts needed to be recalled by the later descendants of these pioneers who would have heard, rather than seen, the great power of God. They were every bit as prone to disregard calls to loyalty and obedience as their ancestors had been. Stories that uncovered the natural tendencies of the human heart required to be repeated and recalled as a timeless message from God. When the people had settled in the land they would then begin to fear deeply the possibility of its loss. At such a time the very fervour and urgency of Deuteronomy's call to maintain love and obedience towards God would begin to sound like a call to a hopeless quest. If the human tendency to unbelief and disobedience was so strong, was not God's law itself more a curse than a blessing? In such a light we could understand that the intense demands to love God which Deuteronomy presents could bring on a feeling of despair. Was not such a summons to love God an impossible demand, since human beings could not meet the fulness of its claims?

This splendid exhortation and reflection offers the answer to such despondent fears. Its watchword is found in verse 19: 'Now choose life...'. Life and all the richness of its promise remained a real and serious reality for Israel to choose. The key feature that made this choice possible is set out in verses 11–14. God's way is not beyond human reach! It is not a great mystery that has to be fetched from a far distant land, nor a heavenly secret that only a special divine messenger can procure for us. No—'the word is very near you; it is in your mouth and in your heart' (v. 14).

4 The living law and living leadership   *Read Deuteronomy 31:9–29*

We have seen how remarkably prominently the person of Moses figures in the book of Deuteronomy since his is the authority that undergirds it all. Yet the book is not centrally about Moses as a person, but rather Moses as the lawgiver of God. In reality it is the law of God that holds centre stage and Moses becomes important since his is the authority which makes it unique and his leadership in the wilderness years makes his exhortations especially relevant. As in all the chapters of the epilogue of Deuteronomy 27–34 we recognize that years have passed since the days of Moses. A new generation is recalling with added poignancy the triumphs and achievements that Moses brought, but which appear increasingly to be mere memories of a glorious past. So again here we have many details included of the trials, temptations and failures that beset Israel when they sought to live out God's way in the land promised to them (note especially verses 16–18, 29). Had

Moses not led them to expect blessings and security which they could not reasonably expect to hold on to?

The answer to such unexpressed fears is given with directness and clarity and implies a resounding 'No!' Israel could continue to enjoy the fruits of Moses' labours because he had made provision for all future generations by giving to them the written law of God. It had been written down and handed over for safe keeping to the levitical priests. Through them it could be read and re-read at the end of every seven years (vv. 9–13, 24–26). So later generations of Israel would readily know the teaching of Moses.

Yet it was not the law alone that mattered, since a continued tradition of national leadership was also required which would see its role as maintaining the nation's loyalty to God which Moses had built up. So Joshua's commissioning also was vitally important (v. 23), since he stood as representative of the continuing line of civil officials and judges who would take their place beside the levitical priests. Moses lived on in the law book he had given and the lines of officials and judges that he had commissioned.

5   A prayer for the future   *Read Deuteronomy 33:1–29*

We speak of Israel as a nation, and so it was for a part of its history during the biblical period. Yet it was not a united nation in our modern sense for more than a very brief period. The sense of Israel's oneness, however, was very important and needed to be kept alive in spite of the many pressures and surprises brought on by new events. It was in large measure the shared faith in the Lord as God, the recollection of the common origin from slavery in Egypt, the indebtedness to the leadership of Moses and the law of God, which established that unity.

In other respects the tribes were very different in their separate characters. The lands they occupied varied remarkably from lush sub-tropical profusion in the north, in the region of Dan, where even lions roamed (a fact echoed in verse 22), to the desert of the far south. Prospects differed greatly so that Zebulon and Issachar in the Phoenician hinterland could benefit from maritime trading (v. 19), whereas Joseph would depend on agriculture and 'the best gifts of the earth' (verse 16).

In this beautiful prayer of blessing for the future the tribes of Israel are reviewed with all their distinctness and varied characteristics. Moses reminds each of them that, with their different gifts, they were nevertheless each indebted to the same God. He calls upon them all to maintain their common obedience to the divine law which belonged to 'the assembly of Jacob'.

So much of the fascination of human community lies in the great variety of skills and attitudes that are contained within it. Part of the wonder of life lies in the great mixture of opportunities that it brings to us. This Blessing of Moses both revels with exuberant delight in this variety, yet strives to keep in the forefront the underlying faith in a God-given spirit of unity. It compares in its spiritual insight with Paul's reflections on the variety of spiritual gifts in 1 Corinthians 14:6–12.

6 I have let you see it   *Read Deuteronomy 34:1–12*

This final chapter of the book of Deuteronomy is also the final chapter of the five books of Moses which begin with Genesis. Together they make up the 'five-fifths of the law'. There is necessarily a note of poignancy and loss since Moses' death marked the end of the era in which Israel received its charter as a nation. No wonder therefore that Israel spent thirty days weeping for the loss of their leader (v. 8). This people would never again be quite the same without him.

In another sense, however, nothing had really begun at all, since the crossing of the River Jordan and the settlement in the land had still to take place. The working out for Israel of what it meant to live under God's law and to assume a place among the community of nations still lay in the future. It is the books which begin with Joshua and continue to the end of 2 Kings which tell the story of how that enterprise unfolded. It is, as the careful reader quickly becomes aware, a far from comforting tale. Disobedience, idolatry and the whole mix of human ambitions dim the shining splendour of that first sight of the land. Yet Moses appears as so much more than an ordinary leader—he was a prophet, in fact a visionary and prophet like no other in Israel (v. 10). The fact that he had seen the land with his own eyes, but had been prevented from crossing into it (v. 4) has remained a key theme, or type, of the Old Testament. The true riches of faith are to be found in what can be seen and envisioned as a goal for the future, not as something that can be quickly and readily grasped. It is a goal yet to be realized. So it was for the readers of Deuteronomy in ancient times and so it remains for the Christian. We have not yet reached the goal of all that the Bible promises. There remains still a task of spiritual taking possession to be accomplished.

GUIDELINES

The book of Deuteronomy forms a charter for Israel as a nation. There is a carefully chosen significance in its presentation as a speech addressed to a nation who were about to take possession of their land. Life as a nation was about to begin and required a proper plan. So, with its inevitable limitations as a relatively brief and summary constitution, it nevertheless singles out the most vital factors that bring greatness to a people and a rich quality of life to those who live within it.

Can you pick out from the passages studied a particular list of requirements for a nation? Is it helpful to make such a list, or do we rely too heavily upon others to choose these requirements for us? There are some remarkable and unexpected features in Deuteronomy which we can reflect upon. In telling the story of the greatness of Israel's birth as a nation it puts great weight on the fact of unbelief and the fewness of those who dared to obey God. It recognizes that the majority of Moses' contemporaries failed to listen to him or to obey God's challenge. Do we pride ourselves too much on the achievements of our national past and forget its failures? In what ways may this also be true for ourselves as Christians?

Can I now draw up a prayer list for my nation, using what I have learned from Deuteronomy to show what are the most needed qualities for God's will to be achieved? Above all is not the emphasis that Deuteronomy puts upon the centrality of each individual's love towards God something that I still need to learn? How can I help others to see that this matters so much?

Acts 13–28

In the first twelve chapters of Acts, we read about the spread of the church which was fuelled by opposition. From its beginnings in Jerusalem it has reached Judea, Galilee and Samaria—but not without some surprising turns. One of its leading opponents, the Pharisee Saul of Tarsus, has become a follower of the Way, and the Gentile Cornelius and his household have embraced the Christian faith. Saul, now called Paul, and the much-respected Barnabas have been sent from Jerusalem to encourage missionary work in the cosmopolitan city of Antioch, where we pick up the story once more.

JUNE 9–15   JOURNEY INTO THE UNKNOWN: ACTS 13:1—15:35

1   The missionary movement is born   *Read Acts 13:1–12*

Antioch 'was a church where worship was central, and where fasting was an indication of their earnest determination to seek God's will. It was a church which cared so much about fellowship that Jews and Gentiles converted to the faith broke down centuries-old barriers and ate at the same table. It was a church where an aristocrat like Manaen, an ex-Pharisee of the most rigid type like Saul, Barnabas an erstwhile Levitical landowner in Cyprus, Lucius a Hellenistic Jew from Cyrene, and "Simeon the swarthy", almost certainly an African, could all work together' (Green, page 218).

It was from this church that 'missionary work' was launched as a church enterprise, following a church decision under the guidance of the Spirit. The missionaries would be representatives of a church, expected to report back on their activities (14:26–28), though not apparently funded by the church.

Why Cyprus? One wonders who suggested Cyprus as a starting point. There were Cypriot members in the church (11:20), Barnabas and John Mark had roots there, but did Paul feel frustrated? Later he shares his ambition to 'preach where Christ was not known' (Romans 15:20), and from Antioch tantalizingly there lay the good Roman road west into Asia Minor. Cyprus already had its Christian churches. Perhaps Luke reflects Paul's priorities in dismissing the early visits

(vv. 5, 6) and focusing on the main challenge of Cyprus, the Roman proconsul himself, who was possibly of a distinguished and cultured family, and wanted to hear the new teaching. This was more like it! Here was Paul's element. The Roman name 'Paul' now replaces Saul (v. 9) and henceforth Paul takes the lead.

Why was Sergius Paulus interested? The Roman authorities always tended to be nervous of Jewish travelling preachers. They could be freedom fighters stirring up trouble (see 18:2). Clearly however the proconsul had 'religious' inclinations, including in his entourage a Jew who, in spite of Jewish prohibitions, practised magic, perhaps in order to tell the future and give advice. Such practices were not unusual (18:18–19).

2 To the Jew first *Read Acts 13:13–52*

The journey to 'Antioch of Pisidia' (there were sixteen Antiochs in the ancient world) took the missionaries a hundred miles inland, first over a vast swampy plain and then up a lonely and dangerous mountain road to a 3,600 feet plateau. John Mark went home. Did he resent Paul's assumption of leadership? Or was he unprepared for such hazardous travelling? We do not know. The conditions may have taxed even Paul to the full, since he was clearly an ill man in these regions (Galatians 4:13–15). William Ramsey suggested he had malaria.

The plan of campaign Paul's strategy begins to emerge:

- He always aimed for key cities, from which the message could spread into the surrounding countryside (v. 49). Antioch and Lystra were Roman military centres on an east-west road; Iconium, a Greek commercial centre down a side road.

- He usually began where he would find people, both Jew and Gentile, with hearts prepared by the Scriptures—hence the significance of the synagogue.

- He grasped the obvious opportunities. After the opening prayers in a synagogue service there was a reading from the Law (Genesis to Deuteronomy), and one of the prophets (Joshua onwards, with the Writings—1 Chronicles to Song of Songs—forming a different section). Then anyone obviously knowledgeable could be invited by a synagogue president to explain the passage (cf. Luke 4:16–21).

- *Paul was aware of a specific prior commission to the non-Jews (Acts 9:15; Galatians 2:2–9).*

- *However it was always a matter of principle for him to share the message with Jews first (Romans 1:16). They were God's chosen channel and Paul cared about his own people (Romans 9:1–4). Today it is sometimes alleged that the Jews know the true God through the Old Testament and do not need Jesus. Paul of the Acts and letters strongly disagrees. In verse 43 he urges interested Jews that the way to 'continue in the grace of God' is to accept Jesus.*

Sermons for every occasion There are some good examples in Acts of gospel messages adapted for all occasions: the gospel for labourer-Gentiles; the gospel for cultured Gentiles; the gospel when under attack. Here we have a model sermon designed for Jews (there are strong affinities with Acts 2 and 7).

The review of Israel's history in verses 16–22 points to the continuity of God's plans and the promise of a Saviour 'in David's line'. The story of Jesus is told as fulfilling the promises (v. 23–37). (Some have suggested 2 Samuel 7:6–16 as the reading from the prophets.) The offer of forgiveness is made to all who believe (vv. 38–40). Here it is interesting to detect some very Pauline language. Alongside the promise of forgiveness, he usually includes law-court pictures with words like acquittal, vindication, the pronouncement of righteousness (justification). With verse 39 compare Romans 3:21–31.

We need the whole Bible There is an increasing tendency today for Christians to ignore the Old Testament. But the Bible is a unity: 'the New is in the Old contained; the Old is by the New explained'. The Bible may be reviewed as a book with the answers at the back! But answers have only limited value if we do not know the question!

3 Miraculous signs and wonders   *Read Acts 14:1–10*

'Am I not an apostle?' (1 Corinthians 9:1). Luke was a great admirer of Paul. Was he concerned in this half of his book to show that Paul had equal standing with Peter and the other apostles? Some may have disputed this. So Luke contends:

- *Did Peter heal a lame man? So did Paul (v. 8f).*

- *Did Peter raise the dead? So did Paul (20:9f).*

- *Was Peter delivered from prison? So was Paul? (16:22f).*

- *Was Peter's presence thought to have special power? (2:15) So was Paul's (9:11).*

The title 'apostle' is reserved by Luke primarily for the twelve appointed by Jesus, but in this chapter is used twice of Paul and Barnabas (vv. 4, 14)

Miracles then and now Jesus' earthly ministry included 'teaching with authority' i.e. accompanied by great power (Mark 1:27). He gave the disciples power to heal and deliver. So in Acts we continue to see the power that went with the proclamation of the message. The emphasis was not on the healer, nor on the miracle itself, but on Jesus and on God's authentication of the truth of the message (v. 3). This continued into the second and third centuries. The early Christian writers are full of it. 'Those who are in truth Christ's disciples, receiving grace from him, do in his name perform miracles... Nor does [the church] perform anything... by incantations or any other wicked or curious art; but by directing her prayers to the Lord... and calling on the name of our Lord Jesus Christ, she has been accustomed to work miracles for the advantage of mankind' (Irenaeus, *Adversus Haereses*, from the second century).

Today in Western society there are well-authenticated examples of exorcisms and healings. But the most striking examples come from the younger churches where there is 'only a tiny church in a vast pagan stronghold... on the fringes of gospel outreach' (Green, page 233). Thirty-one-year-old pastor Illia (Elijah) in Siberia was discussing how he wanted to plant a church in the village of Spaask. He said he would go into the village, preach about Jesus, and pray for some sick people. They would be healed and a church would be started! That was how his currently 200-strong church began, according to the report of Revd Ewen Huffman, in 'The London Bible College Old Students' Newsletter'.

4 First encounter with pure paganism   *Read Acts 14:11–20*

Culture shock Outside Lystra stood a temple to Zeus, and there is archaeological evidence for the cult of Zeus and Hermes. Once upon a time, so the legend went, Zeus (or Jupiter, the 'father' of the gods) and his messenger, Hermes (or Mercury), had disguised themselves as poor travellers and come looking for shelter among the rich and poor in the Lycaonian region. They were repeatedly turned away until they knocked at the door of an old peasant couple, Philemon and Baucis, who welcomed them. Then they revealed themselves, turned into frogs those who had rejected them and transformed the couple's cottage into a gold and marble temple. It was believed that one day those gods would return to be treated with honour.

The responses therefore to the healing miracles here occasion no surprise. The people of Lystra were not being caught out twice! For Paul and Barnabas the shock was probably greater because initially they did not understand what was happening (v. 11). Despite the change in the people's mood, disciples were made (vv. 20, 22; 16:2).

Transposing the gospel There may not have been a synagogue in Lystra, though there were obviously some Jewish residents, such as Timothy, who was Jewish on his mother's side (16:1). The inhabitants were probably largely uneducated farmers. The message to them had to be couched in somewhat different terms. Here is (and more fully in 17:22–31) an example of the gospel to rank outsiders. We notice:

- *no direct reference to the Old Testament (though its thought is reflected. See Isaiah 44:9–20; Psalm 115:4–8).*

- *an attack on idols: 'worthless things' translates 'nothings' in both Greek and Hebrew.*

- *instruction about the one true God, Creator, Sustainer and Provider for people everywhere, and merciful to their ignorance.*

- *the call to 'turn'*

There is no mention of Jesus here, but it might be assumed that Luke is simply giving us what is new to the proclamation. The 'good news' followed as usual.

'Evangelism is never proclamation in a vacuum; but always to people, and the message must be given in terms that make sense to them' (Green, page 138). What do outsiders today need to hear first?

5 'You foolish Galatians!' *Read Acts 14:21—15:1*

Pisidia, Pamphilia and Lycaonia (13:13–14; 14:6) were the original names of ethnic regions before the Romans appeared on the scene. The Romans however divided their empire into bigger slices and Antioch, Iconium, Lystra and Derbe were in the southern part of the Roman province of Galatia. Paul's letter to the Galatians was therefore written to Christians in these cities.

A crisis not mentioned by Luke After Paul and Barnabas had returned to Antioch, their home church, Peter had visited and rejoiced to be part of the mixed Jew–Gentile fellowship, all acknowledging Jesus to be their only hope of salvation. But he had been followed by Christians from Jerusalem, who had formerly been Pharisees and were scandalized by the situation. They insisted that Gentile converts must be circumcised and obey the Jewish regulations. And they were so persuasive that first even Peter and then Barnabas wavered.

Paul however was adamant. The very gospel was at stake—'repent, believe, and be forgiven', not 'repent, believe, be circumcised, keep the law and be forgiven'. Paul won the day (see Galatians 2:11–16). Later however, messengers brought Paul the news that these Pharisee-Christians had gone on to Paul's recent mission field, telling the Gentile believers that Paul had got it wrong and persuading them to accept the Jewish conditions.

Paul's reaction Paul was horrified, and the result was the most impassioned of all his letters. His emotions completely got the better of him.

- *'I am astonished that you are so quickly deserting the one who called you by the grace of Christ'* (Galatians 1:6).

- *'If anybody is preaching to you a gospel other than what you accepted, let him be eternally condemned!'* (1:9).

- *'Who has bewitched you?'* (3:1).

- *'Did you receive the Spirit by observing the law, or by believing what you heard?'* (3:2).

- *'I fear for you, that I have somehow wasted my efforts on you'* (4:11).

- 'What has happened to all your joy?' (4:15)

- 'If you let yourselves be circumcised, Christ will be of no value to you at all' (5:2).

There are no greetings at the beginning or end of this letter! Paul was too upset. Some have suggested that Paul regretted leaving these new Christians so quickly. In his later work, where possible, he stayed for a much longer time.

6   A general synod   Read Acts 15:2–35

The problem, however, would not go away. It required more than one man's indignant, if fully justified, campaign. A ruling was needed from the church's leadership as a whole.

Put yourselves in Jewish shoes   The feelings of these Jerusalem Jews are understandable. They could have put their case in this way.

- *There is a theological problem here. Did not God make a covenant with the Jews, with circumcision as its seal, and promise that through the Jews the world would be blessed? (Genesis 12:3; Isaiah 2:2–3) Has God now changed?*

- *We never envisaged such an influx! And many are straight out of paganism with pagan morals. How can we prevent our Jewish/Christian principles from being contaminated or swept away all together? We need to insist on the law of Moses.*

- *Never in my life have I eaten pork, or meat with the blood in it. Even the thought makes me feel ill. And what if the meat was offered in a pagan temple before coming to the market place?*

These are weighty arguments. But these points carried the day:

- *In the Cornelius event God himself made clear his purpose. He bestows his Holy Spirit on those who respond in faith to Jesus Christ. That alone is required for salvation (v. 11). The experience of Barnabas and Paul bear this out. (Note that in Jerusalem Barnabas resumes the lead.)*

- *Theologically, just as God previously called a people for himself— the Jews—so now he calls a people from the Gentiles (vv. 14,*

17—'Gentiles who bear his name'). It was never God's purpose to make the commandments a requirement for salvation: 'We failed anyway' (v. 10). The Old Testament rightly understood confirms this. 'Rebuilding David's fallen tent' (v. 16) does not refer to the restoration of Judaism, but to its successor, the church. (James is credited here with radical reinterpretation of Amos 9:11–12, but Jesus himself had led the way: see Matthew 21:41–43.)

• *However, courtesy demands respect for other people's scruples. In a mixed table fellowship the Gentiles should be careful what they eat and serve.*

But there are problems with the implication of verses 20. 'Sexual immorality' is not to do with food and can hardly be classed with things which might offend scruples. Some think that it refers to the Jewish forbidden degrees of marriage. Paul in his letter to Gentile churches never mentions as such the requirements of verse 20, but it surely cannot be said that he did not agree with the spirit of them. In many places he majors on sexual morality (e.g. 1 Corinthians 6:12f), and he discusses at length the question of offending others' scruples (1 Corinthians 8; Romans 14).

GUIDELINES

Breaking through the cultural barriers Acts 15 illustrates for us the enormous cultural barrier that lay between Jewish and Gentile Christians and the way in which the earliest church began to address it. Many different kinds of cultural barriers are to be found in the churches today, including age, gender, class, church affiliation and country of origin. So ask yourself:

• *Are any of these found in my church?*

• *What side of the barrier do I stand on, and what are my personal feelings?*

• *What are the thoughts and 'gut feelings' of those on the other side?*

• *Is gospel truth involved, or is it just a matter of custom and habit?*

• *Does the Bible say anything about the issue?*

- *Where might positive public discussion of the issue take place (as opposed to private brooding or group complaining!)?*

- *What might I concede to the scruples of the other side?*

Turn your thoughts into prayer.

JUNE 16–22 JOURNEY INTO EUROPE: ACTS 15:36—19:41

1 Christian teamwork   *Read Acts 15:36—16:10*

When Paul later wrote to the Philippian church he urged them to be 'one in spirit and purpose', and pleaded with two dedicated Christian women leaders to 'agree with each other in the Lord' (Philippians 2:2, 4:2). But the fact is that people are different and sometimes their distinctive gifts and insights will conflict. Paul and Barnabas faced a common problem. What should take priority: the pastoral needs of an individual (Mark, who probably needed a gentler introduction to missionary work), or the progress of an important but exacting work? Their decision to separate was probably right, without, one hopes, lasting bitterness. We hear no more of Barnabas, but Paul later enlisted Mark again (Colossians 4:10; 2 Timothy 4:11).

Paul believed in teamwork, so for his next journey he took Silas, a noted leader and prophet in Jerusalem (15:22). Paul also believed in taking trainees, so *en route* he collected Timothy, who with his grandmother Lois and his mother Eunice, was probably converted during Paul's ministry earlier in Lystra. He commissioned him by the laying on of hands (2 Timothy 1:6) and also had him circumcised. If Jews married Gentiles (though this was officially forbidden) their children were regarded as Jews and circumcision was expected. Paul fought against circumcision seen as a requirement for salvation, but accepted it as part of Jewish culture and wanted Timothy to be acceptable to Jews. There was a further addition to the team in Troas. In 16:10 for the first time the narrative speaks of 'we', most naturally understood as the writer, Luke, joining the expedition. He possibly remained in Philippi (16:40), but rejoined Paul on his return to Jerusalem after the third journey (20:5). Titus also later became an important team member (2 Corinthians 8:16f), but strangely Acts never mentions him.

Note that in 16:6 'Galatia' refers to the ethnic region in the northern part of the Roman province of Galatia. Paul never went there.

2 Paul in Macedonia   Read Acts 16:11—17:15

Was Paul anti-women?   It is often concluded (because of passages such as 1 Timothy 2:9–15) that Paul had a low opinion of women. But due weight must be given to the contrary evidence. As Paul preached the gospel it was frequently his experience that women of influence and great standing responded. This was the case at Thessalonica (17:4) and Beroea (17:12). Some of them became valued co-workers with Paul (note all the women mentioned in Romans 16). Lydia was just such a woman. She was a business woman, running an agency for selling the famous purple cloth from Thyatira on the other side of the Aegean sea. She was perhaps a widow and her household (v. 15) would have included house and business slaves. She was a powerful woman and with her new Christian joy prevailed on Paul and his company to accept free hospitality. (Paul usually preferred to pay his way.) Her house became a centre for the new church.

The power of the message   Today's passage illustrates the different ways in which the Lord convinces the human heart.

• *Lydia's heart simply responded to the message, as the disciples' hearts burned on the Emmaus road (Luke 24:32).*

• *The jailer had clearly heard the message (v. 30), but its impact came home to him, probably on hearing Paul and Silas' 'joy in suffering' (v. 25), on feeling the shock of the earthquake and on seeing the 'miracle' of the prisoners' still being there!*

• *The Beroeans were thrilled with the message, but wanted to be sure it had solid foundations in the Scripture (17:11). A daily study session was necessary and proved fruitful.*

Roman law—friend or foe?   In Philippi for the first time Paul confronted a Roman situation. The city prided itself on being a 'little Rome' (v. 21: 'us Romans'). Its magistrates, though probably native Philippians, were expected to administer Roman justice.

Where Jesus is proclaimed supreme Lord, he will touch not only hearts but also pockets and vested interests (cf. Mark 5:16–17;

Acts 19:25f). So Paul and Silas find themselves dragged to the place of justice by the enraged owners of the slave girl. According to Roman law, the magistrates should have listened to the specific charges, ascertained who Paul and Silas were, and submitted their findings to a higher court for trial. In fact they probably realized that there was no case to be heard (what are the unlawful customs in verse 21?), but wanted to appease the complaints. Hence the flogging and prison for the night. Then Paul and Silas were simply released. By contrast, in Thessalonica, proper court procedures were followed.

In 1 Peter 2:20 we read 'if you suffer for doing good and you endure it, this is commendable before God. To this you were called'. Was Paul right in demanding an apology? Was he following the example of Jesus or not? Yes: he did not abuse or retaliate; he endured the unjust punishment. And perhaps there is an important principle here. If Christians find themselves at the mercy of an unjust system, they might only hurt themselves by fighting it *on their own account*. But Roman justice principles, especially for citizens, were in the main fair and good. Then it is right to ask that justice is done. Paul probably also wanted the new Christian community of Philippi to be treated with respect. This underlines what some have seen as one of Luke's themes in Acts, that in the eyes of the Roman authorities the Christian church was blameless and therefore not deserving of opposition.

3 Paul in Athens   Read Acts 17:16–34

Light from the epistles   The impression is given that Paul rather reluctantly found himself in Athens. The response in the Macedonian churches has been overwhelming, despite the short time that he had been there. Philippi had sent gifts to Paul when he was in Thessalonica and continued to support him (Philippians 4:14–19). The new Christians in Thessalonica and Beroea fearlessly proclaimed their new faith despite immediate and fierce opposition. Paul longed to go back to encourage and strengthen the church in Thessalonica, but after a short stay in the mountain refuge of Beroea accepted the offer of guides by sea to Athens. Silas and Timothy were left behind to help, and rejoined him in Corinth (18:5). All this is vividly documented in Paul's first letter to Thessalonica written from Corinth (see 1 Thessalonians 1:4–10; 2:17–18; 3:1–8).

'Waiting' in Athens   Though bereft of his team, Paul was 'provoked' into activity (v. 16). Rome may have been the capital of the empire but

Athens was the symbol of its religion and culture (albeit lacking its earlier glory)—a city of temples, topped by the Acropolis and the Parthenon with its marble pillars, its famous frieze and the colossal statue of the goddess Athene. The expert craftsmanship of these and other statues and buildings can still be admired today, but in Paul's time they were inextricably connected with false beliefs and rituals and were thus repulsive to him.

Ironically Athens was also the home of philosophical debate, which rejected the pantheon of gods and goddesses. Stoics argued for life in conformity with a kind of 'life force' or 'Reason'; Epicureans advocated a worry-free life of pleasure, with the gods either non-existent or far away! This too probably 'provoked' Paul. He had a Greek education and could enter into intellectual argument. His views however were regarded as strange, and perhaps dangerous, so, like Socrates 400 years earlier, he was brought before the Council. The result is a second but more profound 'gospel for the Gentiles'.

A different gospel Paul's speech has been the source of endless controversy. He appears to commend his opponents—'very religious' (v. 22)—and imply that they could find God by their own efforts (v. 27). Their problem is ignorance, not sin. He quotes their poets, not the Old Testament.

In fact however this abbreviated speech is a masterly example of starting where people are (vv. 24–29), and blending philosophical and Old Testament thinking. The true God is transcendent, immanent and personal; Creator, Controller and Sustainer. But verse 30 makes the crucial point that he is also Judge, so that repentance is called for. Judgment will be dependent on response to a divinely appointed human being, now raised from the dead. Characteristically the intellectual mind struggled with the concept of eternity leaving its footprints in time: this was 'foolishness to the Greeks'.

4 Paul in Corinth   *Read Acts 18:1–17*

Encouragements It is likely that Paul, in making his plans, did not envisage moving from place to place haphazardly. Wanting to found strong new churches, he probably hoped for long 'incumbencies'. However regularly he was forced to move on, he may have arrived in Corinth in a despondent frame of mind. He was alone, he feared for the Macedonian Christians, and although Corinth was a strategic centre, he must have wondered whether the same pattern would emerge (v. 6). He encountered instead the God of encouragement.

- *Two new friends, already Christians, who shared Paul's occupation (leatherworking), gave him hospitality and were destined to become key co-workers.*

- *The arrival of Silas and Timothy with news that the Macedonians were standing firm, and personal gifts which enabled Paul to evangelize full-time (v. 5).*

- *A home to meet in when the synagogue became hostile.*

- *A direct word from the Lord.*

- *A respected and impartial Roman governor, brother of the famous Roman philosopher Seneca. Gallio, unlike Pilate, declared openly that the controversy was a Jewish affair and refused to be manipulated. The Jewish accusation is not clear, perhaps that Paul was fomenting unrest such as had led to trouble in Rome a year or two earlier (v. 2).*

Sosthenes was probably known to be a Christian (1 Corinthians 1:1).

Corinth The new town of Corinth (the old city was destroyed in 146BC) had a population of a quarter of a million, many of them slaves serving a thriving trade, crossing the narrow neck from northern to southern Greece and from the Adriatic to the Aegean seas. It was a cosmopolitan and permissive city, overshadowed on its precipitous hill by the great temple of Aphrodite, goddess of love. A thousand gifts were consecrated to her and sex of all kinds was glorified. It is probably significant that Romans 1:21–32 was written from Corinth.

5 'I planted, Apollos watered' (1 Corinthians 3:6)
Read Acts 18:18—19:7

This could be seen as a 'furlough' period for Paul. He travels from Corinth to Caesarea, with a brief stop in Ephesus. He probably visits Jerusalem and then returns to base in Antioch. The third journey begins in verse 23 with a return visit to South Galatia, before going on for a three year stay in Ephesus (19:1), his other main centre of activity.

Thanksgiving for a completed mission One way for a Jew to express his gratitude to God was to take the Nazirite vow. While in Corinth Paul must have made this act of dedication, allowing his hair to grow. Thirty days later, in accordance with ritual, at Cenchreae, Corinth's port, he shaved his head and then needed to complete the ritual by offering it with a sacrifice in the temple at Jerusalem. Paul was adamant that Jewish traditions should not be imposed on Gentiles, but there is nothing strange about his treasuring those inherited traditions for himself (cf. 21:23f). Messianic Jews today would understand this perfectly.

God's fellow workers Aquila and Priscilla (Priscilla is usually given pre-eminence) were Jews who must have become Christians in Rome. Roman history records the expulsion of Jews in AD49 (18:2), as a result of Jewish/Christian conflict. Aquila and Priscilla came first to Corinth, but then accompanied Paul to Ephesus, perhaps to establish a spearhead for Paul's future plans. A church was established in their house (1 Corinthians 16:9). Later they seem to have returned to Rome (if 1 Corinthians 16 originally belonged to Romans—a disputed issue).

Apollos Christianity had also reached Alexandria in North Africa, though this passage is a reminder that from the beginning it sometimes took shallow or defective forms. It is not made clear in what way Apollos' teaching was inadequate. It could be that, though filled with the Spirit, his teaching on the subject was weak. The twelve men in Ephesus seem to represent a different problem. There is gospel evidence that some of John the Baptist's followers did not accept his testimony to Jesus (John 3:25–26), and such men later became a John the Baptist sect. The group in Ephesus needed Jesus first. Apollos had the special gifts of eloquence and Jewish evangelism and went on to a fruitful ministry in Corinth. It was not his fault that Paul was compared unfavourably with him (1 Corinthians 1:10–12; 3:4–9). Some suggest that he might have been the writer of the letter to the Hebrews.

6 Three years in Ephesus *Read Acts 19:8–41*

Artemis of the Ephesians Ephesus was the first city of Asia and its huge temple of Artemis was one of the seven ancient wonders of the world. It had 117 Ionic columns, each weighing fifteen tons. 'Cities throughout the province of Asia contributed a carefully graded hierarchy of virgins and priests, and a steady stream of visitors who traded, worshiped and returned home with little silver or terracotta replicas of the image of Artemis to watch over their homes' (Pollock). In the spring there was a great festival, the Artemisia. Paul planned to use this opportunity for his work before leaving Ephesus. The success of his mission was shown in a slump in sales (v. 27).

More light from the epistles Luke has chosen only a selection of incidents from this, Paul's longest project. His letters fill out a very crucial period.

- *The Corinthian church was claiming time and effort. News of sexual problems started a correspondence (1 Corinthians 5:9–11). Then a delegation came with news of serious difficulties (1 Corinthians 1:11). In addition to writing 1 Corinthians Paul seems to have paid a disastrous visit and written a stiff letter from Ephesus (2 Corinthians 2:1–4).*

- *Paul was training evangelists to work in the surrounding area. One such was Epaphras, who founded a church at Colossae nearby, (Colossians 1:7). No doubt new Christians travelled into Ephesus to listen to Paul in the 'lecture hall' (v. 9). (One text of Acts states that he taught between 11.00 and 4.00, siesta time, during the hottest part of the day, when the 'school building' was not required and even slaves could attend.)*

- *At some point in Ephesus Paul faced a major crisis. He despaired even of his life (2 Corinthians 1:8). Aquila and Priscilla risked their lives for him (Romans 16:3). Was he imprisoned? Did he face the threat of the arena (1 Corinthians 15:32)? Many scholars have suggested that Paul wrote Philippians from prison in Ephesus. Why did Luke not mention Paul's crisis? Some suggest that the event was politically sensitive. During that time Nero became emperor and the Roman proconsul in Ephesus, Silenus, was poisoned on the orders of Nero's mother. This put at risk all Silenus' party and any whom he had protected, perhaps including Paul. As Paul's apologist it was wiser for Luke to cite the theatre incident than Paul's imprisonment and discharge.*

Magic powers If the curse of Corinth was sexual sin, the curse of the region of Ephesus was the fear of evil powers. This was so potent that exorcism and sorcery became big business. In the wider Roman world documents of spells and magic formulae were known as 'Ephesian letters'. This brought two dangers:

- *that Paul would be seen as a magician and the name of Jesus a magic formula;*

- *that Christians would not completely let go of their fears.*

In spite of verses 18–19 the churches continued to be tempted by fear to deny Christ his rightful place. See Ephesians 6:12 ('our struggle [is] against the spiritual forces of evil in the heavenly world') and Colossians 2:10 ('Christ, who is head over every power and authority').

GUIDELINES

Every chapter has reminded us of the magnetic effect of the good news as people from every stratum of society welcomed the new faith.

- *What was so attractive?*

- *One of the glories of the gospel is its power to satisfy so many needs, not surprising of course when we consider that its source is the living God, revealed in Jesus, in whose image people are made, and therefore our 'hearts are restless till they find their rest' in him (St Augustine).*

- *As in the ministry of Jesus, the message was music to the ears of society's disadvantaged. It brought dignity and self-respect to know oneself accepted by the Father God, who also knew the meaning of undeserved suffering. In a world where many felt oppressed by the power of evil and trapped by unavoidable and indifferent fate, the gospel brought deliverance. Jesus was the lord over all, his power was demonstrated, his friendship available. For those seeking the truth, the gospel made sense of the universe, offering not just abstract philosophy but a personal spiritual encounter. The Christian community itself exercised a powerful attraction: changed lives, joy and enthusiasm, practical love, high moral standards.*

Think

1. *Why am I a Christian? What first drew me and what continues to inspire me?*

2. *What elements in the gospel and the church might draw people today?*

JUNE 23–29 JOURNEY TO JERUSALEM & ROME: ACTS 20–28

1 'To Jerusalem, compelled by the Spirit' (20:22)
     Read Acts 20:1—21:17

Luke now leaves the subject of Paul's pioneering work, simply recording the route of the third journey (vv. 1–2). These last chapters, though clearly important to Luke, are perhaps the least well-known and seem strange. Why such detailed geographical information? What part do the trial reports play? The hazardous sail to Rome is fascinating, but what is it saying?

In the steps of the Master Earlier in Acts we noted how Luke often saw the life, death and resurrection of Jesus re-enacted in his followers. Perhaps this is one clue to Acts 20–28. Paul 'resolutely set out for Jerusalem' (cf. Luke 9:51). He was arrested and tried by both Jews and Romans. He was declared innocent (Acts 26:31–32). Is resurrection life symbolized in the journey to Rome?

From Corinth to Jerusalem While in Corinth Paul wrote his letter to the Romans, obviously longing to go on there—and further (Romans 15:23–25). Previously each journey had ended by returning to Antioch. But this time Paul's goal was Jerusalem. Why?

• *All Jews were encouraged to be there for major festivals. Paul's change of route (v. 3) meant that he missed Passover (v. 6), but he was determined to make Pentecost (v. 16).*

• *Throughout his ministry Paul had endeavoured to unite Jew and Gentile in one church. The mother church in Jerusalem, predominantly Jewish, had still not truly faced the issue (21:20). Paul took representatives from the new churches to illustrate the work of God (v. 4). From his letters, but omitted by Luke except at*

24:17, we know too that each church was sending a generous donation (Galatians 2:10; 1 Corinthians 16:1–4; Romans 15:25–27). Paul recognized the important principle of mutuality in mission.

Farewell meeting The journey to Jerusalem is punctuated by reunions and prophecies that hard times lay ahead. Paul's address to the Ephesian elders (vv. 17–35) can be seen as a general farewell to the churches. Classical literature contains many such speeches and the words have a Lukan flavour, but there is no reason why it should not represent Paul's words. Luke was there. If the speech is genuine, verse 25 must mean that Paul did not intend further work in this area. His sights were set on the western Mediterranean. He is not forecasting certain death (v. 22). Some scholars however see here Luke's knowledge that Paul had already died when he wrote these words. See the notes in Day 6.

2 Paul's arrest—a peace-making gesture gone wrong
Read Acts 21:17—22:29

'*To the weak I became weak*' (1 Corinthians 9:22). 'Weak' Christians according to Paul are those who, while trusting in Jesus for salvation, still need the security of fixed rules and traditions. Otherwise their consciences suffer. Such may have been the condition of many Jewish Christians in Jerusalem who were 'zealous for the law'. (Alternatively they were compromising in order to avoid confrontation with their fellow Jews.) Paul's principles are helpful. He gloried in the freedom which enabled him to assess the significance of traditions and distinguish essential from non-essential, but he was not 'in bondage to emancipation' (Bruce). He would not knowingly offend the sensibilities of others (see Romans 14).

It is unlikely that Paul had ever advised Christian Jews to abandon the practice of circumcision, but no doubt some, with their new freedom, rejoiced in their wider understanding of 'God's chosen people' and counted circumcision unnecessary. As a conciliatory gesture Paul agreed to stand alongside the four men under a Nazirite vow and pay for the sacrifices. He himself had earlier valued this rite (18:18). The only puzzling feature here is the reference to 'purification rites'. The Nazirite ceremonial did not require any special cleansing act and in any case Paul was not here involved in the vow himself.

Some suggest that he submitted to cleansing from Gentile defilement, required before entering the temple. But would Paul have gone that far (see Acts 10:15)?

Paul's gesture Ironically the very attempt to pacify Jews becomes the occasion for a Jewish attack. No way would Paul have taken any Gentile beyond the notice in the temple threatening death to any foreign intruder! But Ephesian Jews, in Jerusalem for the Pentecost, had seen Paul with Ephesian Trophimus and assumed that the four men were Gentiles.

Paul, defender of the faith In the next five chapters Paul changes his role from missionary preacher to 'apologist' (in 22:1 'defence' translates *apologia*; see also 24:10, 25:8, 26:1f, 26:24). He does not simply answer charges against himself but witnesses to Jesus and the gospel. In the same way Nelson Mandela defended himself by proclaiming the human rights message.

No doubt Luke again is giving us his own dramatic presentation, but the speeches are characteristic of Paul. The basic message is that Judaism should lead to faith in Jesus as Messiah, because of the resurrection, but the speeches have appropriate variations according to circumstances. Here Paul, accused of defiling the temple, details his impeccable Jewish background and commitment; uses the Hebrew (or Aramaic) language; cites the support of Ananias, a devout and respected Jew; and describes his commissioning by Jesus in the temple itself.

3 Trial before Jews   *Read Acts 22:30–23:34*

A defence document? How are we to read these incidents? Is Luke, as some say, writing a document for the defence of the Christian Church, or even of Paul in Rome? This and the following chapters would certainly make the points:

- *that implacable hatred drives the Jews who oppose Paul (vv. 12–15; 24:27—25:3);*

- *that the Romans were kindly disposed towards Paul (vv. 16–34);*

- *that if there was a specific charge against Paul, it was purely Jewish and not a state matter (23:29; 25:19);*

- *that even the Jewish charges were unclear and unsubstantiated (25:27) and the original accusers have disappeared (21:29; 24:19);*

- *that Paul has done nothing worthy of death or imprisonment (23:29; 25:25; 26:31).*

As in the case of Jesus, the Jews try to convert a religious charge into a political one, but are even less successful with Paul.

Or a thrilling Christian biography? Paul is Luke's hero and Luke has a gift for dramatic story-telling. This could be another key to the rest of the book, always recognizing however that it is 'his-story'—Jesus' story. Out of total confusion the Lord *will* get Paul and his witness to Rome (v. 11).

Notice the drama in Luke's account here:

- *Paul is human! He feels frustrated by the turn of events (v. 1) and loses his temper (v. 3). This sheep is not dumb (cf. Isaiah 53:7)! An attempt to preach the gospel ('It is possible to be a Pharisee and a Christian') goes horribly wrong (vv. 6–7). Surely Paul did not intend to stir up a hornets' nest.*

- *A nephew comes from the wings! Many of Paul's family must have treated him as if dead for his apostasy, but there were believers among his relatives and some believed before he did (Romans 16:7).*

- *Paul is given a military guard of 470 men (v. 23), almost half the Jerusalem garrison!*

- *His innocence is recorded in an official document (vv. 25–30)! How did you get that, Luke? Its contents are not a verbatim record (see 23:25 'as follows' means 'to this effect', 'of this type'), but they are perfectly plausible. Lysias the garrison commander skates nicely over his own bungling, when reporting to the governor.*

4 Paul's 'passion'   *Read Acts 24:1—26:32*

Personalities of the passion Jesus' trial brought him before Caiaphas the high priest, Pilate the Roman governor, and Herod Antipas the puppet-king of Galilee, who was just curious (Luke 23:8). What a strange comparison with Paul's experience!

Ananias is described by the Jewish historian Josephus as insolent and quick-tempered. Paul's surprising words in 23:5 could mean 'I did not think a man who could give such an order could be the high priest.' His apology was genuine, but 23:3 proved to be prophetic. Ananias was dismissed in 48 and assassinated in AD66.

Felix and Festus were two in a line of governors of Judea, when the emperors wanted the province under their direct control. They were not high ranking officials since Judea had only minor status, but theirs was a difficult appointment.

Felix was a freedman in the emperor's favour. He was reputed to be violent, and according to the Roman historian Tacitus he 'experienced royal power with the mind of a slave'. Here we see him publicly acting justly by stopping proceedings (24:22), privately with his Jewish wife intrigued by the gospel, but deviously, having failed to benefit financially from the situation, avoiding trouble by keeping Paul in prison.

Festus was a better governor and there is nothing implausible about his desire for Agrippa's advice. He had to refer a prisoner to Nero's court, with nothing to write about the charges!

Herod Agrippa II the son of Agrippa I in Acts 12, had charge of north eastern Palestine. Bernice was his sister and they were nominally Jewish. He always tried to mediate between the Jews and the Romans. Like Antipas he was curious (25:22).

Luke–Acts spans the reigns of five emperors (Caesars)—Augustus, Tiberius, Gaius, Claudius, Nero.

Dramatic dialogues While using historical information available, Luke employs all his dramatic skills in these chapters. Tertullus relies on sickening flattery to cover up a weak argument and inarticulate speech (this is clearer in the Greek).

Paul easily answers the charges:

• *I've only been here twelve days.*

• *I came to worship, not evangelize.*

• *My accusers are not here.*

• *We do not belong to a sect, but the Way (the true way of worshipping God).*

- *In the temple I was ceremonially clean.*

- *I am on trial for my theology.*

Paul's speech in chapter 26 is a brilliant appeal to the Jews, although possibly Agrippa and Bernice were the only Jews present (26:26). Festus is totally unable to cope with the Jewish theology (26:24).

It is likely that Luke deliberately uses chapter 26 for a full summary of the content of Paul's message:

- *The starting point is the Old Testament hope (vv. 6, 7; see also 23:6, 24:15).*

- *The resurrection has confirmed that Jesus has fulfilled those promises, not only as the Davidic Messiah, but also as the suffering servant of Isaiah (v. 23: 'a covenant for the people and a light for the Gentiles'; cf. Isaiah 42:6–7).*

- *All people are called to trust in Jesus, to repent, and to receive forgiveness and a place among God's people.*

5 And so we went to Rome   Read Acts 27:1—28:15

At no other point in Acts are we so aware of the author witnessing events.

Remembering a thrilling but frightening sea journey Adventures at sea have always fascinated people. Luke knew that his account would appeal. He was not a sailor, but he gets his facts straight and gives us a vivid picture of contemporary sailing conditions:

- *regular passages from Egypt to Rome bringing vital corn supplies;*

- *the sometimes larger passenger lists (v. 37): 'Italian and Egyptian merchants, possibly a string of African slaves, army veterans returning on retirement; scholars from the great University of Alexandria; women and children. With all these and a big cargo of wheat the ship must have been over 500 tons' (Pollock);*

- *a typical vessel: 'She had only one large mast carrying a huge mainsail, thus putting heavy strains on her timbers. She was*

steered by detachable rudders rather like large paddles and her
captain had no compass or chronometer and the roughest charts,
so he never knew his position unless he could see sun or stars'
(Pollock);

- *the changeable winds: tacking along the Asia Minor coast to avoid*
  a strong westerly (v. 4, 5); welcoming a gentle southerly as they
  round Cape Malta (v. 13); struck by the dreaded north easterly
  from Mount Ida and riding before the storm (v. 14); aware that
  safe sailing ended perhaps three weeks earlier (v. 9).

- *all the miseries of long weeks in a storm-tossed sea: cramped*
  conditions, shortage of food, creaking timbers (vv. 17–21).

Luke's Greek pride, and ignorance of Roman waters, show through
in 28:2f. He describes the Maltese as 'barbarians'! (What Gentile was
to Jew, barbarian was to Greek), and is surprised by their hospitality.

Marvelling at the presence and power of God in Paul Paul was a
prisoner among prisoners, but from the very first he impressed Julius,
the centurion (27:3, 43). Julius continued to allow Paul a considerable
amount of freedom (28:7, 14). Various facets of Paul's character are
seen. He was allowed a say (27:9), he was susceptible to fear (27:24),
but was granted a further vision from God, which he was eager to
share and won him the respect of the captain and crew (27:31,
33–36). He was recognized in Malta as a man of God. Roman
Christians travelled forty-three miles to meet him and eased some
depression about the future (28:15).

Paul was delivered from death. Some have even described it as a
kind of resurrection. Certainly Luke sees it as a vindication of the
worth of his mission (28:4f), although he is alert to the fact that not
all of Christ's servants will escape violent death (Acts 7:54f, 12:2).

6 'The word of God is not fettered' (2 Timothy 2:9)
   Read Acts 28:17–31

Paul probably arrived in Rome about AD60. These were years when
Nero, under the influence of the philosopher Seneca, exercised a
moderate rule. The Christian Church flourished, though Luke only
refers to its initial, enthusiastic welcome to Paul. But by AD64 Nero
had become a mad, unpredictable tyrant: he had a section of Rome set

ablaze for 'redevelopment', but then turned the blame on to Christians, carrying out such tortures that even the Roman people pitied them.

What we do not know Did Paul's trial ever take place? Was he in fact condemned to death in AD62 or later? 2 Timothy was also written from prison and if Paul wrote it, he was envisaging his end. Tradition has it that Peter and Paul were martyred at the same time in Rome. But why does Luke not say so? It would have suited his theme. Or had it not happened when Luke was writing? Perhaps Paul was freed after the two-year stint for a further period of ministry. There is a tradition that he visited Spain. Many scholars question whether Paul wrote the pastoral epistles (1 and 2 Timothy, Titus), but if he did, he was free when he wrote 1 Timothy and Titus and they do not fit into the Acts' travels.

What we do know Paul had his privacy, and no doubt his guard profited (28:16)! Large numbers had access to him (v. 23). This picture of Paul's Roman ministry can be filled out from his letters. Colossians was written from Rome (Colossians 4:7–18). The slave Onesimus had found his way to Paul and carried the letter to Philemon back to his master in Colossae. Ephesians come from Rome (Ephesians 6:10–24), and perhaps also Philippians (Philippians 4:21–22).

A major theme in Acts has been the unstoppable progress of the gospel. This chapter is a fitting conclusion, and verse 31 rounds it off. Even Paul's being under house arrest cannot hinder the working of God's Spirit. Christians should never feel that useful ministry is denied them by the restrictions imposed in this world.

GUIDELINES

A missionary prayer session

Think

- *In your local church where are the outreach opportunities? Who are the key leaders?*

- *In what other area of the world do you have a special interest?*

- *Are you giving to any particular project or missionary society?*

- *Does your church have missionary partners? Do you know their names and what they are doing? Be honest with yourself. Are your prayers of the 'Please bless Richard and Sheila in South America' type?*

Listen to Paul's prayer requests, as if from the lips of your own missionary link.

Philippians 1:4—I always pray with joy, because of your partnership in the gospel.

Colossians 4:3-4—Pray for us... that God may open a door for our message and that I may proclaim it clearly.

Ephesians 6:19f—Pray that I may declare the gospel fearlessly as I should.

2 Thessalonians 3:1—Pray that the message of the Lord may spread rapidly and be honoured.

Romans 10:1—My heart's desire and prayer to God is that they may be saved.

Pray that your missionaries may have opportunities to witness, find the right words (remember language and culture) and not be afraid. Also that they will encounter prepared hearts (like Lydia's), and that people will be converted.

Romans 15:30f—I urge you to join me in my struggle. Pray that I may be rescued from the unbelievers and that my service may be acceptable to the saints.

Pray for the protection in opposition and wisdom in working with national Christians.

2 Corinthians 1:8—We were under great pressures, far beyond our ability to endure. Help us by your prayers.

Pray about the special pressures your missionaries face.

1 Timothy 2:1—I urge that requests be made for everyone, for kings and those in authority (remember Paul's experience).

Pray for national Christians and about contacts with national authorities.

Follow Paul's example, when he prayed for Christians.

Ephesians 3:16f—I ask God to give you power through his Spirit to be strong in your inner selves. May you come to know his love and be completely filled with the nature of God.

Colossians 1:9f—We ask God to fill you with the knowledge of his will so that you are able to endure everything with patience.

Risen and ascended Lord, deepen our understanding of your great love for your servants everywhere; deliver us from self-concern and make us channels of your grace to those for whom we pray, to the glory of your name.

For further reading

F.F. Bruce, *Paul, Apostle of the Free Spirit*, Paternoster, 1977

Michael Green, *Evangelism in the Early Church*, Hodder & Stoughton, 1970

I.H. Marshall, *Acts*, IVP, 1980

John Pollock, *The Apostle*, Hodder & Stoughton, 1969. This is written in the form of a historical novel, but sticks closely to the New Testament text and brings the journeys to life.

Nahum and Obadiah

It's best to come clean at the outset and admit that the books of Nahum and Obadiah are not everyone's favourite bedtime devotional reading. Indeed, more than that, for some people they confirm their worst fears about the Old Testament. It is often alleged that the Old Testament is a book about judgment, war and hatred of people who are to be annihilated in God's name, while the New Testament is a book about the love, grace and compassion of God for all. Most readers of these *Guidelines* will know that such a view is a gross over-simplification, but the books of Nahum and Obadiah might seem to lend some credence to it.

Both books seem to be an unapologetic gloat over the defeat of Israel's enemies. The enemy in Nahum's case is Nineveh, the capital city of Assyria, one of the great oppressor nations who attacked and ill-treated both the northern kingdom of Israel (which it conquered) and the southern kingdom of Judah. Nahum either predicts the fall of Nineveh or rejoices in its capture by the Medes in 612BC (it is not always easy with the Hebrew prophets to know whether they are foretelling something which is yet to happen and which they regard as so certain they can speak of it as though it has already occurred, or whether they are referring to a past and known event). Whichever Nahum is doing, he is drawing considerable satisfaction from the contemplation of Nineveh's fate.

For Obadiah the enemy is Edom. The Edomites are singled out for particular treachery against Judah, and this little book (of only 21 verses) also gloats over the fate which awaits them. In neither book does there appear to be any hint of criticism of the people of Israel and Judah themselves as there is in most other prophetic books. The sins the other prophets so roundly denounced go apparently unmentioned here. Both books therefore seem to typify the worst kind of national-ism and exclusivism.

It is always difficult to date the prophetic books of the Old Testament. Nahum refers to two historic events, the capture of the Egyptian city of Thebes by the Assyrians (which happened in 661BC) and the fall of Nineveh itself (612BC). The original prophet Nahum (whoever he was) may therefore have prophesied during the second half of the seventh century BC. It is clear, however, that the tradition about each prophet went through a long process of development before it crystallized into the present form of our prophetic books and, as time went on, particular historical events may have gained symbolic significance, just as the author of the New Testament book of Revelation can refer to Rome as 'Babylon'. It is even more difficult to date Obadiah, but scholars have usually thought he prophesied after the fall of Jerusalem in 586BC when the Edomites were considered to have helped the Babylonian armies, either by attacking Judah themselves or, at least, by doing nothing to help them. A good deal of resentment against the Edomites appears in the post-exilic Old Testament writings.

As we read we shall have to ask ourselves whether we can find anything in these books which is more than sheer xenophobic hatred and lust for revenge. Can there be any word of God of enduring value and relevance which comes through them? The notes are based on the Revised Standard Version of the Bible.

---

30 JUNE–6 JULY   NAHUM 1:1—OBADIAH 21

---

1   God is sovereign and righteous   *Read Nahum 1:1–8*

Verse 1 is the kind of heading which later editors have given to all the prophetic books. The name 'Nahum' means 'comfort' but we know nothing else about the prophet, even the name of his town is uncertain. For later editors and readers it was not the prophet but his message and its continuing relevance which mattered. They say his oracle concerns Nineveh but, as we shall see, much of it is of considerably more general reference and, by the time of this heading, when the prophet's words can already be spoken of as a 'book', 'Nineveh' may have become a symbol of all that is opposed to God's will.

Verses 2–8 form a vivid poem (the poetry of this book is of superb literary quality) in which the first letter of each verse begins with a different letter of the Hebrew alphabet in order (an 'acrostic'), running from 'a' to 'k' (half the alphabet). The 'k' of verse 8 begins the Hebrew word 'to make a complete end'. Extraordinarily, the poem draws on many motifs familiar to us from Canaanite poetry with its descriptions of Ba'al. Indeed, in verse 2 three names for God appear, 'Yahweh' (the nearest we can get to the Hebrew name for God), 'El', used of Yahweh but also the name of the supreme God in the Canaanite pantheon, and 'Ba'al' where the Hebrew idiom says that Yahweh is 'lord (*ba'al*) of wrath'. His power both in ordering creation out of chaos and, when necessary, in reversing that process in judgment, is what is being hymned. Yahweh is the God who embodies all the powers of heaven and earth in himself.

However, he is not only the God of wrath and judgment against all and everything which opposes his righteous and sovereign purpose (vv. 2–3) but also the God who loves to be merciful and who is 'slow' to anger (v. 3, which quotes the great covenant promise of Exodus 34:6). He is also 'good' and a protection for all who trust him (v. 7).

This opening poem actually says nothing about historic 'Nineveh' at all. It hymns the sovereign power and utter goodness and reliability, the grace and compassion of God. He must ultimately sweep away all which opposes his 'good' purpose in his universe. Far from being just a hymn of hate against foreigners, it announces to all readers that it is open to us whether we experience God as judge or as saviour.

2 Good news for the oppressed   Read Nahum 1:9–15

Today's passage contains a number of passages of alternating threats of judgment and promises of deliverance. Whichever English translation we use it cannot help disguising an extraordinary variety in the Hebrew where we have reference to other people in third person speech (e.g. vv. 10, 12a, 13), and direct address in the second person (vv. 9, 11, 12b, 14, 15). Yet even in this last case there is a variety of 'you's' addressed: singular and plural, masculine and feminine. This may all be because it is comprised of a good deal of familiar prophetic material (compare v. 15 with Isaiah 52:7, for example). It may also be due to the desire of later editors to extend Nahum's words to the wider audience of their own contemporaries. And here we should note the very broad, general themes of prophetic teaching which are included here. The absurdity of human plans and programmes when they run counter to God's own purposes (vv. 9–11) can be found in many places in the prophetic books (e.g. Isaiah 10:5–19, also directed against the Assyrians). Similarly, the worship of false gods and images (v. 14) is widely condemned, not least when the Israelites themselves are guilty of it (e.g. Hosea 13:1–3). All this lifts the general indictment and warning of the book of Nahum above a mere diatribe against one city and one people to a warning against such wickedness wherever it is found.

There is also in today's reading a promise held out to the oppressed and afflicted (vv. 12–15). This is nothing unusual. Isaiah 40–55 is full of such promises to the exiled Israelites, and other prophets promise God's justice for those who have been wronged by the powerful, the wealthy and the evil. Again, this is more than just the promise of a deliverance from a particular enemy. It is a promise that God will judge all oppression and wickedness because he is on the side of its victims, wherever they are to be found.

3 Evil judged *Read Nahum 3:1–11*

Today's reading does link the theme of God's judgment of evil with a particular city, Nineveh (v. 7), and she is compared with another city which the Assyrians themselves sacked, the Egyptian city of Thebes (v. 8). But again, there is plenty of evidence to suggest that these have just become 'typical' of all those sins in human society which God intended to root out. This is far from being merely a xenophobic hymn of hate against a particular group of foreigners.

The opening poem (vv. 1–4) beginning with the word 'Woe' takes the form of a funeral dirge or lament, a form familiar in the prophetic books. It is as though the prophet is joining in the lament of those who attend the funeral of the city and its inhabitants. Its fall to the sudden attack of a ruthless army is vividly and dramatically portrayed (vv. 2, 3). But note the reasons for the attack. It is a 'bloody' city, full of the blood of innocent victims; its foreign and domestic policies have been based on deceit and betrayal; it has grown rich as its storehouses have become full of merchandise plundered from others. Further, it is attacked for its religious falseness, for the repeated term 'harlotries' would have only one overtone for Israelite hearers. It was the term used repeatedly by the prophets to attack Israel's own betrayal of Yahweh by turning to the worship of other gods (e.g. Hosea 4:12–15; Jeremiah 3:1–3; Ezekiel 16:15–22). This theme is developed in the verses which follow, as though it is of great importance for those responsible for the final form of the book, the idea of 'harlotry' being continued in the picture of the public shaming of the woman who is guilty of it (cf. Jeremiah 13:26).

Other themes from Israel's prophetic tradition are also found here. The Hebrew word in verse 6 rendered in the RSV as 'I will throw *filth* at you' means literally 'detestable things', a word often used of Israel's idols (e.g. Jeremiah 7:30). The boasted strength of a nation and its trust in its foreign alliances which Thebes is said to have shown (vv. 8–9) will never be enough to withstand God's judgment (v. 10; cf. Isaiah 10:5–19). 'Nineveh' herself will also know just such a fate (v. 11).

The attack of this book against 'Nineveh' then, turns out to be an attack on those sins against God and humanity of which Nineveh was later seen to be a typical example. Whatever the exact force of the original message, it is now used as a warning to any who indulge in the same sins. God judges and saves, not according to nationality, but according to how nations and people ally themselves to, or oppose, his purposes of justice for all.

4 The futility of human pride   *Read Obadiah 1–9*

Today's reading provides an example of the very close parallels which sometimes exist between one piece of the Old Testament and another. It forms a kind of poem which contrasts Edom's geographical situation, high up in easily fortified mountain clefts and strongholds, proud of its military security and strength and of its cultural achievements, one of which is the prowess of its 'wise men', with the fate God has in store for it, its utter overthrow and downfall.

Verses 1–5, however, are very close indeed to Jeremiah 49:9, 14–16, where almost the same words are also directed against Edom. Most scholars these days do not talk in terms of one prophet 'copying' another. It is far more likely that both draw on a common source and there are many who think that, especially with material like the books of Nahum and Obadiah, such a common source may well have been in Israel's worship. It is worth pointing out when we are thinking of the allegedly rather nationalistic nature of these books that, in fact, all the major prophetic books have a section devoted to oracles concerning foreign nations (e.g. Isaiah 13–23; Jeremiah 44–51; Ezekiel 25–32). These usually express the 'judgment on the oppressor nations and so salvation for Israel' theme. It is quite possible that these had their original home in Israel's worship in the temple and were intended as a means of *securing* the defeat of their enemies and deliverance for themselves. The books of Nahum and Obadiah may be examples of just such material which did not become attached to a larger collection. But if there was something of a common stock of such material that would explain the overlap of vocabulary and themes such as we have here.

Certainly the themes of the overthrow of human 'hubris' is a familiar one in the Old Testament. It is the theme of the story of the building of the tower of Babel in Genesis 11:1–9. It is a frequent motif in Isaiah, especially with his repeated refrain, 'For the Lord of hosts has a day against all that is proud and lofty, against all that is lifted up and high' (e.g. 2:12). Not Edom's position (v. 4), nor its vaunted 'wisdom' (v. 8) nor its mighty army (v. 9) will prevail against God who will see that Edom falls because of the very same kind of treachery (v. 7) which they have shown to others.

5 A failure of care   *Read Obadiah 10–14*

The Old Testament presents a complex picture of the relations between Judah and Edom. An ancient tradition believes they were related, especially in the stories which show Jacob and Esau as brothers (although, as is often the case with brothers, their relations were often tense, Genesis 25:19–24; 27:1–45). Obadiah draws on this tradition, 'your brother Jacob' (v. 10), 'the day of your brother' (v. 12). Elsewhere there are some strong hints that the worship of Yahweh originated from the territory of Edom (Judges 5:4; Deuteronomy 33:2) and Deuteronomy has a special word calling for concern for the Edomites (23:7). A long history of cruel warfare between the two showed that this was by no means always observed, on either side.

So the alleged treachery shown by the Edomites towards Judah could fit quite a number of occasions in their history but most scholars believe this does refer to the time when the Babylonians finally invaded Judah and laid siege to Jerusalem, destroying it in 586 BC. The post-exilic literature showed that the iron entered deep into the Judean soul at what was thought of as either Edom's inaction in offering any help to Judah or her active assistance of the Babylonians (although they are not mentioned in this way in 2 Kings 24:1–2).

Perhaps it is wrong now to ask questions of our text about precise details of history, however. In yesterday's reading we saw how 'Edom' had become almost a symbol of the loftiness of human pride. Today we see it as an example of the failure of care between 'brothers'. This is another Old Testament theme, well illustrated by Cain's question to God when he had killed Abel, 'Am I responsible for my brother?' (Genesis 4:9). The Old Testament has plenty to say about those who fail to see in the unemployed, the poor, the immigrant, the oppressed, the one who is 'my brother'.

Today's reading offers a climax to all that has gone before in the little book of Obadiah and, in some sense, to all that we saw in Nahum. We note, first, that the horizon has widened. Esau is certainly mentioned (vv. 18, 19, 21) but the 'day of the Lord' is coming upon 'all nations' (v. 15) and other traditional enemies of Israel are also specified, the Philistines (v. 19) and the Phoenicians (v. 20). This adds further weight to the idea, already apparent from our earlier readings, that 'Esau/Edom' has here become a symbol of all Yahweh's enemies, of all that is opposed to his purpose for righteousness in the world.

Those who have done wrong by oppressing others will now themselves be oppressed (vv. 15, 16). Indeed, God will use the weak, now fired by his strength and his zeal, as the agents of his judgment (v. 18), just as much later St Paul would say that God uses the 'little people' of the earth to confound the 'mighty' (1 Corinthians 1:26–31). Those who have been dispossessed (v. 13) will now possess what is rightfully theirs (v. 17). The security and holiness of Mount Zion (v. 17), to which either those who have been saved (as some Greek MSS have it) or those whom God will use as 'deliverers' shall go up (v. 21), contrasts in a powerful climax with the false security and injustice of the mighty rock fortress in which the Edomites dwelt, described at the beginning of the book.

But this is not just a hymn of vengeance. It does not suggest that there will be simply a reversal of roles in which Israel will reign as supreme power, rich on what they have plundered, in place of Edom. They will be instruments used by God to establish his rule, and they will again possess what is rightfully theirs, but, ultimately, 'the kingdom will be the Lord's' (v. 21). He will rule, denying all forms of evil, from whomever it comes, the power to oppress and subjugate. When he reigns, everything of which 'Edom' had become a symbol will be overcome. But for those whom he has delivered, the place of his rule will be 'holy'. His kingdom offers no freedom of the city to those who want only their self-interest in place of the interest of others.

GUIDELINES

We may catch something of what those who arranged our Old Testament found to be the lessons of our two books by thinking about their place in the canon. Obadiah immediately follows the book of Amos. For all the threats of judgment in Amos the final chapter does offer hope, and many scholars think that Obadiah may have been placed where it is because it was seen as a kind of commentary on Amos 9:11–12:

> *In that day I will raise up the booth of David that is fallen*
> *and repair its breaches, and raise up its ruins,*
> *and rebuild it as in the days of old;*
> *that they may possess the remnant of Edom*
> *and all the nations who are called by my name, says the Lord who*
> *does this.*

Both Amos and Obadiah testify to the reality of a God who judges sin, intent on purging his creation of all injustice and oppression. Yet both testify to a real hope based on his grace and his power to save those who turn to him.

In the Greek Bible (the Septuagint) Nahum has been placed after Jonah. Some have pointed to a number of parallels between the two books, both about the same length, both dealing with the fate of Nineveh, both centring on the great covenant declaration of Exodus 34:6 and, most interestingly, both ending with a question. Nahum ends with a rhetorical question addressed to Nineveh, 'For upon whom has not come your unceasing evil?' Jonah ends with God's question to his distraught prophet, Jonah, angry at God's apparent care for Nineveh: 'And should not I pity Nineveh...?' Again, taken together, the two books witness to the fact that God works towards his purposes of justice and righteousness on earth in both judgment *and* mercy.

If we could dismiss both Nahum and Obadiah as mere diatribes of hate it would be very convenient because they would then present us with no challenge. But if, as we have seen, original words about particular places have been extended to challenge us about where we stand in relation to God's purpose of justice for all, they turn out to be far more searching—and disconcerting.

For further reading

R.J. Coggins and S.P. Re'emi, *Israel among the Natio...
Obadiah, Esther*, International Theological Commen...
and Handsel, 1985

R. Mason, *Micah, Nahum, Obadiah*, Old Testament Gu...
Press, 1991

Paul wrote that, I'll eat my hat': thus traditionally did a famous ew Testament professor begin his lectures on the epistle to the ebrews. For the authorship of this epistle has been a puzzle that has eased the minds ever since the time of Origen and Tertullian in the hird Christian century. Almost certainly it was *not* written by Paul, but intriguingly it overlaps with several of his concerns. Then again, particularly in the first chapter, Hebrews seems to echo ideas expressed in the Gospel of John. Yet taken as a whole Hebrews stands unique in the New Testament. It is an eloquent and sustained argument or 'word of exhortation' (Hebrews 13:22), reflecting on both the significance of the person and work of Christ and its consequences for the Christian believer, and making use of titles and images which appear nowhere else in the New Testament.

Perhaps it is the uniqueness of Hebrews that has led to its being undervalued in recent times. The language of priesthood and cult with which the author wrestles feels obscure and arcane to us in the Western world of the late twentieth century. Yet if Hebrews is neglected, that is our loss, for the author manages to hold together the glory of Christ's divinity and the painful reality of his humanity in a manner that can provide both vision and inspiration.

When I was asked to write these notes on the epistle to the Hebrews, I was both attracted and somewhat daunted. It was an opportunity for me to look at the way in which the New Testament writers used the Old Testament—which is one of my own special interests. But though I have always been intellectually fascinated by the epistle, previously I had found it rather emotionally cold. In part this is because as a letter whose author and recipients are both unknown, it seems anonymous, lacking a full human context. As I began to explore Hebrews, however, resonances of the story of Stephen, the first martyr of the Church, about whom I had been recently writing, kept coming to mind. And though certainty about the authorship of the epistle will always elude us, there are sufficient links with the ideas of Stephen and his group of Greek-speaking Jewish Christians to make it plausible that one of the 'Hellenists' of Acts, perhaps a friend of Stephen himself, is responsible for this work.

So I have decided to 'read' Hebrews through the eyes of those early Jerusalem Hellenists: to contextualize the author by suggesting that he may have been one who witnessed Stephen's fate, and himself suffered in the persecution that followed Stephen's death. You could find it helpful, therefore, to glance at the story of Stephen in Acts 6–7, and if you happen to have them to hand, to look briefly at the notes on that part of Acts which appeared in *Guidelines* May–August 1990. The 'cloud of witnesses' of Hebrews 12:1 shines with a peculiar intensity if among its luminaries are not only the great figures of the Old Testament history but, implicitly, one who was the author's near contemporary and even friend. The Bible version referred to is the RSV.

7–13 JULY   HEBREWS 1:1–13

1   In the image of God   *Read Hebrews 1:1–4*

A mirror of God The world of the Old Testament and that of the Greek philosophers coalesce in these few verses, to open the epistle with power and paradox. We are led back through the prophets to the story of creation in Genesis 1, and to the 'word of power' and the wisdom with which God then brought all into being. We are being reminded too that humanity was itself made 'in the image and likeness of God' (Genesis 1:26), for strange though it may seem to us, that is what ultimately lies behind the description of the Son as the reflection and 'very stamp' of God. These are terms coined to express with particular intensity the likeness of Christ to God, suggesting that in the Son the invisible Father can be glimpsed by human eyes, yet they also implicitly remind us that to be a mirror of God's glory was the end for which all humanity was brought into being.

A Greek Genesis But the Genesis to which we are led is an Old Testament viewed through the spectacles of the great philosopher Plato, and perhaps also his Jewish disciple, Philo of Alexandria. Philo based his thinking on the Platonic assumption that the material word merely consisted of imperfect copies of 'ideas' which existed in incorporeal reality. He suggested that Genesis 1 related the creation of 'ideal humanity', while the humbler yet more graphic picture of Genesis 2, where men were fashioned from the dust of the earth and women from the side of men, tells us of the making of early 'copies' of human beings. These are imperfect, yet even in their shadow form they reflect something of the glorious ideal and original intention of their Creator.

Glory unmarked So it seems that our writer is presenting the Son as the epitome of humanity, but of humanity as the Ideal it was always meant to be. In us the image of God is marred and stained, in Christ, creation's heir, it shines with a radiant splendour. Our problem then is not that we are too human, but that we are not fully human enough. In learning from Christ what it means to be human, we may begin to reflect his glory and be changed into his likeness. It is possible the martyr Stephen has shown us how. For as he died he saw the glory of God, and his face became like that of angel (Acts 6:15; 7:55).

2 My well-beloved Son *Read Hebrews 1:5–14*

Angels are immortal. They neither marry nor are given in marriage, nor do they suffer death. That was part of the common understanding of Jewish thinkers of the period.

Christ indisputably died: on the cross, a particularly shameful and degrading form of execution. As elsewhere in the New Testament, the scandal of the cross forced upon the Church a re-evaluation and development of traditional theology and received wisdom.

Higher than the angels Angels are fascinating—they help us to provide the poetry of our faith. They are also dangerous, for they help to distract us from mundane realities. Angel worship exerted a seductive pull over some early Christians (see Colossians 2:18). Alternatively, other believers seem to have regarded Christ himself as a kind of angel, one among others. The necklace of different Old Testament quotations which has been strung together here is fashioned to give the lie to both ways of thinking. The Son is infinitely superior to and qualitatively different from angels; why venerate lesser beings? How can the Son who died be one of the angelic immortals? His death, far from witnessing to his failure, has become the means and proof of this uniqueness among those in heaven (1:4, 2:9).

A suffering Son Significantly, the title 'Son' is the one that reverberates loudest in this chapter. It could mean different things to different people, a fact that was both opportunity and danger. The phrase 'son of God' appears quite often in the Old Testament to denote a heavenly being, one who could also have been called 'an angel' (see for example Psalm 89:6). So when our author states so forcefully that the Son is far superior to angels (vv. 5, 13), he was perhaps seeking to counter this traditional belief which may have been common currency among his readers. But the expression 'son of God' was also used of the kings of Israel, at least from the time of David. Since the Messiah was regarded as David's heir, eventually the Messiah also was called 'son of God'. That seems to be the understanding that underlies most of the Old Testament quotations in this chapter, since they come from the royal psalms of David. But there is one other resonance of the phrase 'son of God' which should not be forgotten. It is a note that will become more apparent as the epistle develops. The association between Jesus' sonship and his obedience is an underlying current: it is in doing his Father's will that the Son reveals his true nature. Once upon a time Adam had been called 'son of God' (see for example Luke 3:38), but he had lost the right to this title because of his disobedience: now the Ideal Adam regains this honour as the pattern of disobedience is reversed and undone.

3 Lower than the angels *Read Hebrews 2:1–9*

The pioneer of the persecuted Perhaps those of us who live in western Europe sometimes hold an idealized view of the position of Christians in situations of persecution. The blood of the martyrs may be the seed of the Church, but we also learn from the parable of the sower that seed can wither when oppression occurs. My life in Lebanon taught me something of the mind- and body-numbing quality of fear. Fear seems to have been the lot of those for whom this author was writing. It had them in such thrall that backsliding from their Christian faith was a serious possibility. That is the problem which is here being addressed. The answer? A reminder of past power and future glory. Is Stephen the witness implicitly referred to in verse 4? Back in Acts 6, the wonders and signs that he performed are particularly noted, and the fact that he was filled with the Holy Spirit is emphasized (Acts 6:3, 5, 10). The link is certainly possible. If so, the story of Stephen, the follower, reinforces the truth that can be learned from hearing about the Lord, who travelled the same road before.

The use that is made of Psalm 8 is significant. Once again the ideal humanity of Jesus comes to the fore. In its original context the psalm spoke of the ambiguous place that all human beings hold in the spectrum of God's creation: a little lower than God. But the author of

101

Hebrews, reading the Old Testament in its Greek version, understood this as meaning 'for a little while lower than the angels'. The word 'little' thus refers to time rather than degree. Even though we still await our share in this glory, it has already been achieved by Christ acting on behalf of all other human beings. The little while of suffering is already ended for our pioneer, and ended too for Stephen who seemed to share in the glory of the Son of Man as he too tasted death (Acts 7:56).

4 Perfect through suffering   *Read Hebrews 2:10–18*

Flesh and blood There are few places in the New Testament where the identity of Christ with his fellow human beings is stressed as prominently as it is in these verse. Christ knew fear, knew temptation, knew suffering, knew death. He knows us from the inside out. He calls us brothers, he shares our flesh and blood, he is Son and we are fellow sons with him. The very word 'pioneer' (2:10) emphasizes the fact that though Christ may have journeyed a path before us, it is the same, not a different path that he journeys. Here, as elsewhere in Hebrews, the words 'made perfect' are boldly employed of Christ. The idiom of perfection is one that partly arises from the author's interest in cultic worship. Sacrificial animals had to be 'perfect', complete and without blemishes: so too did those who did the sacrificing. But to speak of Christ being 'made perfect through suffering', as the author does, is to make a paradox of the metaphor: the sores, the cuts, the stinking squalor that made up the ordeal of crucifixion did not destroy Christ's perfection and suitability for sacrifice but rather helped to create it. There is more that will be said later about these words 'made perfect'; they, along with the description of Christ as 'high priest' which first appears in verse 17, are one of the epistle's major contributions to the New Testament.

'My God... remove this cup!' The fear of death which we all experience is acknowledged in verses 14–15. Back in Eden it had somehow been the interaction of the fear of death and the desire for knowledge that had created the first temptation. Christ was not immune from such fear, nor even from temptation, states our writer. It is surely not accidental that Hebrews 2:12 includes a quotation from Psalm 22, one of the most important scriptural tools used by the early Church to understand the meaning of the crucifixion. For the opening words of that psalm: 'My God, my God, why have you forsaken me?',

uttered by Christ on the cross (Mark 15:34), speak with a power that is unparalleled and uncomfortable of the way Christ plumbed the depths of human anguish and desolation in the face of his death.

5 Lead us not into temptation *Read Hebrews 3:1–19*

Waiting in the wilderness Quotations, either explicit or implicit, from the Psalms and the book of Numbers underlie the argument of this chapter. The tiresomeness and recalcitrance of the Israelites in the wilderness after the exodus from Egypt, their moaning and their murmuring, is alluded to at several points in the New Testament. Stephen used the theme as a jibe at the Jewish leaders in his speech of defence (Acts 7:39). Here the accusation is turned instead against some members of the Christian community. The Christian life is a continuing pilgrimage: it may have its beginning in a new exodus, a passing from death to life, but that does not mean that the promised land can be entered straight away. There is a necessary time of proving, perhaps even of temptation, there is a wilderness to be wandered in, which may end by entrapping us. It is at this time that faith, which is the confidence that God can bring to fruition what he has already begun, becomes of supreme importance. It had been lack of faith and trust that had been the undoing of the original Israelites. For the readers of Hebrews, their wilderness time was a period of persecution. If, as is almost certainly the case, the readers were Christians of Jewish origin, the easy course for them must have been to revert to the practice of Judaism, since this was a religion tolerated by the Roman state. Judaism stood for the sure and the known; the very essence of the new faith was that it demanded faith in an unknown future. So in these verses Hebrews begins to address the question of the relationship between Judaism and Christianity which will dominate the following chapters of the epistle. Like Stephen speaking before the Sanhedrin, the author of Hebrews had a vision that looked forward, no matter what it cost: so the Old Testament itself is held to 'testify to the things that were to be spoken later' (3:5).

6 To enter God's rest *Read Hebrews 4:1–13*

'Today' Underlying the argument of these verses is the powerful statement that comes at their conclusion: 'The word of God is living

and active...' (4:12). The 'today' of Psalm 95 to which the author returns in this chapter (v. 7) is not past history but is held to address the readers in the present moment.

There are some quite intricate details in the reading of the Old Testament with which we are now presented. Indeed the fashion in which Hebrews looks at the Old Testament here is quite alien to the way in which most modern readers would do so. The author's basic text is still Psalm 95, which was first introduced in the previous chapter (3:7). On the surface Psalm 95 refers to the episode of murmuring in the wilderness (3:16–19), yet the author of Hebrews believed that the psalm had been written by David—centuries after that incident. So, Hebrews argues, how could the 'today' of the psalm relate back to the wilderness: it must instead be addressing people who come after the psalm was written—namely the readers of the epistle! It is they who are being warned of the danger of backsliding.

Rest Another pivot of the writer's interpretation of the Old Testament is provided by the word 'rest'. He links together the 'rest' of Psalm 95 with the 'rest' of God at the end of creation (Genesis 2:2). But this verse in Genesis presented a logical problem to Jewish scholars. For if God rested, would not the world he had created fall apart? The answer seemed to many that God's 'rest' would only happen completely at the final end of time—the time of endless sabbath. Hebrews (like John 5:17) accepts this solution: rest in a heavenly city rather than an earthly promised land is what still remains as a pledge for this new people of God.

Not Joshua but Jesus Finally, in the reference to Joshua our author leads us subtly back towards Jesus: he, Joshua's namesake (the names are the same in Greek), will be the one who leads the successful pilgrims to their rest and goal.

GUIDELINES

'The glory of God is humanity alive, and the life of humanity is the vision of God.' Famous words from St Irenaeus; though, perhaps tellingly, the first half of the sentence is far better known than the second. In this week's readings we have been learning about Jesus' humanity—and by implication the possibilities inherent in our own. We have heard that the Son is indeed the reflection of God's glory (1:3), a glory revealed not just in Christ's present power and majesty but also 'in the suffering of death' (2:9). We have learned too of the sharpness of God's dealings with his human creation: if we are properly to reflect his nature then we must expect to be pierced and changed by his discerning and purifying sword (4:12).

What does it mean for human beings to be in the image and likeness of God? Did not Stephen learn this before he died?

---

1   Priest of mercy   *Read Hebrews 4:14—5:10*

A gentle priest   As in the story of Christ's passion, so also in the passion of Stephen the high priest had played a crucial role (Acts 7:1). To remember this undergirds the description of Christ's high priesthood with a peculiar poignancy. Christ stands in sharp contrast to the high priest of the Jerusalem temple who knew much of power but little personally of suffering. Surely there is deep irony then, when 5:2 describes how the high priest should 'deal gently' with those whom he represented? For our writer, Christ's very weakness has become a point of strength—his temptations, his experience in Gethsemane, his learned obedience—all coalesce to enable him to fulfil the role of acting on our behalf appropriately and with compassion.

The undoubted allusion to Gethsemane in 5:7 (cf. Mark 14:32ff) takes us to the heart of Christ's fitness for the role of humanity's high priest. There is no other moment in the Gospel narrative where his human dislike for and fear of what lay ahead is stressed so firmly, yet alongside this is set his ultimate acceptance of the Father's will: in Gethsemane's garden the new Adam undoes the disobedience of Eden. Significantly, it seems, both here in Hebrews and in the Gospels, it is because of his painful obedience that Jesus can call God 'Abba, Father', and be acknowledged as Son (see also the notes to Hebrews 1:5–14).

Prayers and tears   High priests offer sacrifices: as the epistle develops we will learn more about the sacrifice that Christ offers. But here we are told that he offered prayers 'with loud cries and tears' (2:7). It was not only his death itself that formed Christ's representative work on behalf of humanity, but in his fear and terror in the garden beforehand, he as high priest summed up the agonies, the painful prayers of our own most desperate moments.

Hebrews explores the depths of Christ's humanity, yet even so verse 9 startles us. Does 'being made perfect' imply that at one time Christ was not? It is a daring statement, but one which acknowledges the reality of the human condition. Our lives are not static; as we grow into adulthood we discover that different responses are appropriate to the ones we made as children. And as we encounter more difficult challenges, our faith and obedience must either deepen or begin to wither. It was only when confronted with the final human test—the fact of death—that Christ's human obedience and perfection could be fully measured.

2 Christ's imperfect followers   Read Hebrews 5:11—6:20

Maturity The 'growth' of Christ into perfection leads naturally to a discussion about the maturity—or lack of it—of the first readers of the epistle. The two themes are intimately connected: in Greek the words 'mature' (5:14) and 'maturity' (6:1) come from the same stem as the word 'perfect' used to describe Christ in 5:9 and elsewhere. Undoubtedly these verses are some of the most difficult in the epistles: the author's condemnation of apostasy as the unforgivable sin has a harshness about it that sits uneasily with his stress elsewhere on Christ's compassion and sympathy with out weakness. Perhaps this explains the apparent relief with which the author switches to commending his readers in 6:9.

The 'elementary doctrine' which our author assumes as a given in 6:1 has a curious ring to it. None of the points listed in verses 1–2 are specifically Christian. They focus not on who Christ is, but rather on what the earthly Jesus might himself have taught. Such 'doctrine' may have been the essence of the first proclamation of the gospel among the Jewish community of Jerusalem. But in reading the book of Acts we realize that the faith of the early Church had to grow and change as it met new situations. To stand still was not to hear the voice of the Spirit.

Staying safe Stephen was perhaps the leader of those who realized this more forcefully. He saw more clearly than the original apostles the question mark the gospel posed regarding the role of the temple. In consequence he was stoned, while those whose faith was slower to develop could remain safe for a while in Jerusalem (cf. Acts 8:1). Our author, Stephen's heir, was aware that to remain with the 'elementary doctrine' could in itself become a temptation; it was so much more comfortable than developing a 'mature' faith, which by expressing its distinctiveness from Judaism laid itself open to persecution, yet true faith must always move forward, no matter what the cost. There is no better example of this than Abraham (Hebrews 6:13–18). Not only was he prepared to journey to an unknown land and future, but he also endured the possibility of the death of his son. His faith, like that of the first readers of this epistle, could rest on no more than trust in God's promise, but that was, or should be, enough. After all, for those like Stephen and our author, whose faith had travelled beyond the temple at Jerusalem, the skies had opened up and the inner sanctum of heaven had been breached.

3   Priest of God Most High   *Read Hebrews 7:1–28*

Abraham naturally leads on to Melchizedek. There are only two places in the Old Testament where Melchizedek is mentioned: in Genesis 14 where Abraham greets him after the victory over the four kings, and in Psalm 110:4. He seems a mysterious figure, and this led to the large amount of speculation about him in Jewish literature of New Testament times. There is even a text to be found among the Dead Sea Scrolls which suggests that some regarded Melchizedek as angelic or divine. It is possible that these ideas have influenced our author. But at least of equal importance was Psalm 110. The first verse of the psalm is quoted back in chapter 1 (v. 13); it was a 'proof text' very commonly used in the early Church to explain the exaltation of Christ at God's right hand. Using the first verse as the starting point, Hebrews, uniquely among New Testament writings, now moves on to reflect on verse 4. It has already been quoted in 5:6 and alluded to in 5:10 and 6:20. For our writer, Melchizedek was an admirable prototype of Christ.

A priestly king   First, Melchizedek was both king and priest. It could be maintained by those who knew Jewish tradition, that if Jesus was of the family of David and thus ultimately descended from Judah (7:14), he was not of the priestly dynasty of Levi and Aaron. How then could he be described as a true 'high priest'? Yet as Melchizedek's heir, Christ can hold together both the royal and the priestly roles that his followers wanted to give him.

Melchizedek and Levi   What is more, he even outranks those of the Levitical priestly families, since Abraham, Levi's ancestor, had long ago acknowledged Melchizedek's superiority. But it is also important that the priesthood promised by oath in Psalm 110:4 was 'for ever'. This promise could only properly be fulfilled by one like Christ who, because he had defeated death, would remain 'for ever'. As chapter 7 draws to a close the full implications of Christ's high-priestly role become clear: his priestly work includes the sufferings endured and the prayers made during his human life, but it does not cease there. Now, ascended in the heavens, he stands as God in the presence of God, and is able, as a priest, to intercede for humanity, and to receive the spirits of those, like Stephen, who die in faith. In consequence, traditional forms of human priesthood become obsolete: all human beings now have equal access to God through Christ. Once upon a time the words 'draw near' described the role of the priests of the Jerusalem temple. Now, in Hebrews (7:19, 25), the phrase can apply to us all, Jew or Gentile, male or female.

4 The true tent *Read Hebrews 8:1–13*

The shadow… Plato's theory of ideas underlies the thought of Hebrews at this point, as it did in chapter 1. The Levitical priests are inferior to Christ, not merely because of their impermanence, but also because they minister in an inferior sanctuary. The earthly tent or tabernacle is only an imperfect copy of the true heavenly tent where Christ's own priesthood is being exercised. The author seeks to underline his point by referring to the book of Exodus.

There (Exodus 25:40) Moses on the mountain is shown a pattern that he is to use for constructing the tabernacle—a statement originally intended to emphasize the importance of the sanctuary that Moses was commanded to erect. But by New Testament times a different understanding of the verse was common. It was held that there was a perfect heavenly sanctuary which Moses had been privileged to glimpse (cf. Revelation 15:5) and that what was later built on earth was a mere 'shadow' of this ideal reality.

… And the substance But our author has also turned the influence of Greek philosophy in a novel, biblical direction. For Plato, the contrast between the heavenly and the earthly, the ideal and the copy, was timeless and permanent. The writer of Hebrews, on the other hand, like other biblical writers, believes in a contrast between the old and the new, this age and the age to come, and also uses the language of shadow and reality to describe this. The old covenant is a mere

shadow of the new covenant whose day is now dawning: as Christians we stand at a point where the old age and the new overlap. Soon, the earthly and old will pass away, and only the new and heavenly remain.

5 A sanctuary not made with hands *Read Hebrews 9:1–28*

The author apologizes for the lack of detail (9:5) he gives us regarding the furnishings of the tent. Some of his modern readers, however, may feel that in chapters 9 and 10 we begin to sink under the weight of the many complicated allusions he makes to sacrificial worship and the tasks of the high priest! They *are* complicated, and it does not help that the various occasions of sacrifice in Judaism—the Day of Atonement, the daily sacrificial offerings, the covenant-making ceremony—have been linked together in a rather undifferentiated fashion.

Both priest and sacrifice It may help to reach the kernel of the author's thought if we remember that he is starting from certain basic 'givens' about the life and death of Christ, and seeking to interpret them in the light of his Jewish heritage. First, Christ died: a freely chosen death by crucifixion, and a death that because it took place at Passovertide was linked in the minds of his followers with a blood sacrifice and a new or renewed covenant. Second, deeply embedded in the earliest traditions of the Church was the awareness that Jesus' attitude to the Jerusalem temple was a major contributory factor to the official hostility towards him: he had both physically attacked the wranglings that accompanied temple business, and verbally predicted its destruction. Both these 'givens' underlie the teaching our author now expounds. The contrast between the earthly and heavenly tents which continues here from the previous chapter draws out explicitly what was implicit in Jesus' own view of the temple. Similarly Stephen had derided the Jerusalem temple as 'made with hands' (Acts 7:48), a phrase that is echoed by contrast here in verses 11 and 24. Our writer seems to have taken the view that the work now accomplished by Jesus in the heavenly sanctuary has rendered the earthly sanctuary redundant. Redundant would also be the word to describe the role of the Jerusalem high priest: for a more perfect sacrifice had now been offered by one who was both priest and victim.

Tent and temple What is striking is that it is two tents rather than two temples that are here compared. After all it was a temple in Jerusalem—not a tent in the wilderness—that our author knew, and from which the Church experienced hostility and withdrew. Yet a tent was movable, and in a temple the deity stood still. Perhaps the somewhat archaic description of a 'tent', which harks back to the book of Exodus, is a reminder that even in the shadowed days of the Old Testament the right way of worshipping God was in a sanctuary which was not fixed in an earthly city: a tent allows God—and God's people—the proper freedom to move forward (compare Acts 7:44–50).

6 Sacrifice and sin   *Read Hebrews 10:1–39*

Why sacrifice? That is the question that dominates chapters 9 and 10. Old and New Testament sacrifices are compared and contrasted: New Testament sacrifice being far superior, because it has offered 'once for all' and does not need repeating. The very fact that the sacrifices of Old Testament days happened 'year after year' shows that they were not able to deal definitively with sins.

Yet even though the sacrifice of Christ is clearly of a different order, one of the author's basic 'givens' is that sacrifice is necessary for the forgiving of sin and to allow human access to God. 'Without the shedding of blood there is no forgiveness of sins' (9:22). Because of this belief he reinterprets Old Testament scripture: the logical understanding of Psalm 40 (quoted in Hebrews 10:5–7) is that all sacrifice is unnecessary and undesirable. Our author, however, has understood it instead as pointing forward to the sacrifice of Christ.

So great a redemption   The idiom of cultic sacrifice is one that does not necessarily come easily to us in the late twentieth century, in spite of the number of hymns that focus on 'the blood of Jesus'. We may feel like asking *why*, if God is all loving and all powerful, there was the necessity for this particular path to be taken in order to achieve the forgiveness of sins. Could not God just have decreed by divine fiat that human beings had free access to himself? Yet, however irrational we may feel the need for 'sacrifice' to be, there is something deep within the human psyche that responds to the costliness which is implicit in acts of sacrifice. We need to know, even if God himself does not, just how painful human sin and alienation is to God... and the sacrifice of Jesus is a prism which focuses this with exquisite and excruciating sharpness.

'A priest for ever'—the priestliness of Christ has been the focus of this week's readings. He is peculiarly fitted for this task because of his intimate connection with God (8:1–2) and human beings (4:15). He is therefore able both to represent God to humanity, and human beings to God. But though the uniqueness of Christ's priestly work is clearly emphasized in representing us before God, there is a sense in which we too are gradually drawn into sharing this representative role towards our fellow men and women. It may involve us in sharing in persecution and suffering (10:32): in this we are intimately identified with Christ and share something of his true humanity.

Stephen, in his death, imitated Christ closely and was refashioned to become part of the Son of Man. Did not his suffering and witness help bring about the conversion of Paul, and through Paul so much of the Gentile world?

21–27 JULY   HEBREWS 11:1—13:25

1   Faith on the journey   *Read Hebrews 11:1–16*

What is faith?   What is faith? It is one of those New Testament concepts that is undoubtedly important, but difficult to pin down precisely. Faith is evaluated quite differently by different writers: Paul's estimate contrasts markedly with that of James. Hebrews seems to be giving us a clear definition (11:1), yet as we read on through the list of the heroes of faith we become aware that there is more to this than is apparent at first sight. The initial statement could be understood as suggesting that faith makes up 'the gaps' in situations where reason is not adequate: faith deals with the unseen and the future.   *present*

Footsteps of faith   Yet as Hebrews gives us specific pictures of what faith means, it becomes obvious that to regard faith as a vague peering into a crystal ball is in itself inadequate. Faith is a relationship of trust in God, that the whole of life and creation is under his control (11:3). It can involve actual acts of righteousness, as in the case of Abel and Enoch. It can mean an acceptance of God's promises, and confidence in his ability to bring them about, however humanly impossible they may seem. But an important part of what constitutes faith for our author is the willingness to sit light to this world, recognizing that since our real homeland is in heaven, any powerlessness or persecution we may endure in the present earthly political order is not of ultimate significance. So Abraham is a hero of faith not simply because of his willingness to journey into the unknown, nor because of his acceptance of the joyful impossibility of the birth of Isaac. The very fact that after finishing his journey from Mesopotamia and entering Canaan he remained a nomadic wanderer, stands as a symbol for faith that is not tied and bound to present mundane realities. Back in Act 7, Stephen had used the story of Abraham to speak of a God on the move who was not constrained by land or place.

Now Stephen's friend demands that the followers of that same God must themselves travel equally unencumbered.

2 Faith in God's future *Read Hebrews 11:17–40*

Suffering We return to Abraham, but now it is Abraham's willingness to sacrifice Isaac, his son, which is praised. The near sacrifice or 'binding' of Isaac has been understood by many Christians as prefiguring the actual sacrifice of Christ (cf. Romans 8:32). It is possible that this thought is also on our writer's mind. As we continue through this second part of the roll call of faith we find ourselves focusing increasingly on willingness to suffer—even death—and hope for resurrection. Through these deeds of courage we are perhaps meant to catch a glimpse of Christ's own: they are foreshadowing the climactic description of Christ's passion and vindication in 12:2. So, for example, we are told, somewhat strangely, that Moses suffered abuse for the Christ (11:26): the hostility that Moses encountered in his mission resembles the hostility that Christ endured in his turn. So too the 'blood' which Moses sprinkled (11:28), even though not his own, resonates with the blood shed when the new covenant was inaugurated. Our author stands in line with Stephen's speech in Acts 7, which also tells of a suffering Moses who is a shadowy precursor of Christ.

Faith's heroes Finally, as the list travels through Israel's past history, it draws to a close by referring to the heroes of the Maccabean revolt of the second century BC. That was a time of particular persecution, when questions of life and death were writ large, when the faithful had little choice but to wander about (11:38), for if they remained in their own towns and cities they would meet certain death. It was the time *par excellence* in Israel's past when people died not because of the vagaries of war and political history, but because they upheld their traditional faith. It was therefore also the time when the question of resurrection—of appropriate reward for the faithful righteous—became paramount. So in the books of the Maccabees we hear the powerful story (2 Maccabees 7), alluded to here in verse 35, of the mother who willingly sacrificed her seven sons in the expectation that she would receive them again in the resurrection. But what is striking is that this episode of Jewish history—and the Old Testament figures mentioned previously—are now claimed as part of the inheritance of the Christian community. By implication this is part of the epistle's response to those who were tempted by persecution to revert to their ancestral Judaism. If this 'cloud of witnesses' surrounds the Christian community, then surely it was only as Christians that believers of the Jewish race could remain in full continuity with their Jewish heritage (cf. John 5:39).

3 The victor in the race   *Read Hebrews 12:1–11*

Triumph over death   The glorification of Christ, seated at the right hand of God, as proclaimed in Psalm 110, is here once again recalled (v. 2). This phrase from Psalm 110 has provided a melodic theme running through the epistle: first introduced in 1:3, it is picked up again in 8:1 and 10:12, and now forms an important bridge between the faithful of history and the frightened of the author's present. Christ seated at God's right hand is testimony to the triumph of resurrection over his—and our—deaths. Christ seated at God's right hand can also intercede with God for those who may be tested by persecution. We are told to 'look to him' for reassurance: remember how Stephen, in Acts 7:55–56, as he was being stoned 'gazed' upon Christ whom he saw at God's right hand.

A father's discipline   Back in Hebrews 1:3 the quotation had accompanied reflection on the sonship of Christ. Here too, it is linked with the theme of sonship: but this time it is *our* sonship that is the subject. This parallelism is no accident; our inheritance as sons and daughters derives ultimately from the work of Christ, his status as Son and his willingness to call us brothers and sisters (see 2:10–11). But as in the case of Christ, sonship carries with it responsibility as well as privilege. To run the race (12:1) we need training, or education. Like Christ himself, we need to 'learn obedience' (compare 5:8). The linkage of 'discipline' with our familial status that is emphasized in verses 5–11 is startling to modern Western eyes: less so perhaps, in the ancient world, where a father had the power of life and death over even his adult children. Perhaps it is useful to remember that the word 'discipline', which appears several times throughout these verses, could equally be translated as 'educate' and 'education': neither discipline nor suffering is an end in itself, but is the means by which human beings are stretched till they reach their full stature and adulthood in the faith.

4 The city of God   Read Hebrews 12:12–29

Journey to Zion Back in the Babylonian exile (c. 540BC) an anonymous writer drew a vivid and inspiring picture of the return of his fellow exiles through the desert to Jerusalem. He called upon images culled from the ancient traditions of Israel's exodus from Egypt: but one thing is missing. That exilic writer, often called the Second Isaiah, did not route the wilderness journey via Mount Sinai. There is no mention in Isaiah 40–55 of that mountain, where laws had once been given, and Israel's failures had begun. By contrast, the only mountain that is mentioned is Zion, or Jerusalem, where grace, not law, awaits, where God will be fully present with his people, and which is the very goal of the journey rather than an ordeal to be surmounted.

This vision, with its implicit contrast between Sinai and Zion, underlies the epistle to the Hebrews. In 12:12 the author quotes from Isaiah 35:3, and then continues by leading his pilgrim readers along the 'holy way', not to Sinai, which is alluded to in verses 18–21, but towards Zion, a place where both angels and humans can fully participate in the worship of the invisible God. There is, of course, a difference between Hebrews and the hopes of the exilic prophet. The Jerusalem of Second Isaiah, though idealized, nonetheless remains located firmly on this earth. Not so for the author of Hebrews: it is a heavenly and invisible Jerusalem which is the goal of his pilgrim party.

O Jerusalem The language of the epistle now takes on a particular power: do we hear in the passion the author's disillusionment with and sorrow for the earthly Jerusalem that he must have known? The seductive symbol of Jerusalem was a two-edged sword: both captivating its lovers by its beauty, and ensnaring them in a web of hatred, of craving for power and possession. In the early history of the

Church the importance of Jerusalem was a crucial question: those like Stephen came to realize quite quickly that Jerusalem and its temple could be a trap that prevented the new faith from travelling—geographically, theologically, and beyond the exclusive boundaries of Judaism. So the earthly Jerusalem must be replaced by the heavenly; but even so, in the image of the heavenly Jerusalem there is a painful echo of what might have been—a city that really was a vision of peace (cf. Luke 19:42), instead of, as so often in its history, a theatre of war.

'Father, forgive' Abel's blood (v. 24) had cried out for vengeance and bloodshed that devotion to the earthly Jerusalem had so often engendered (see for example Psalm 137 and Luke 10:50f). The words uttered at Jesus' death—and also at Stephen's—were by contrast words of forgiveness and reconciliation: appropriate language for a true high priest.

5 A God of fire   Read Hebrews 12:25—13:8

Flame of wrath Is it strange that chapter 12 closes with the words 'Our God is a consuming fire', quoted from Deuteronomy? We have been told in 12:18 that we have *not* come to a tangible, blazing fire. So what is this fiery God that we encounter? Does Hebrews speak enough of God's love? Or at the end of the day is it a picture of wrath that we are left with? There does seem to be a kind of tension that runs throughout the Epistle. On the one hand, there are few parts of the New Testament where Christ's compassion for and solidarity with human beings is stressed as strongly as it is by this writer. On the other hand, there are points where the possibility of Christian failure and the impossibility of a second chance for those who fail is highlighted in an awesome and frightening fashion. And now another contrast confronts us, between the high theology of chapter 12 and the mundane, almost banal prescriptions for behaviour which follow immediately in chapter 13. Some have argued therefore that this last chapter comes from a different hand from the main body of the epistle. Yet, as we shall see, there is enough of a common thread to make this suggestion unnecessary. It is quite normal practice among the writers of New Testament letters to follow up their theological arguments by setting out practical consequences for Christian living (see for example, Romans chapter 12ff).

The same... for ever Perhaps the sentence with which today's reading closes provides our answer. It is an affirmation that despite all appearances the God represented in Jesus Christ is neither fickle nor changeable. His compassion and his wrath are but two sides of the same coin. He is as concerned with the social harmony and spirit of brotherhood in the Christian community as he is with shaking the earth. For if Christians are brothers and sisters of Christ, and in God's image, then to offer hospitality may indeed be to entertain angels unawares.

Flame of love And the image of fire? We picture it in fearsome terms: yet fire warms as well as consumes. It was through the fire of a burning bush that the gracious act of liberation from Egypt began (Exodus 3:2); it was with fire too that the birth of the Church was welcomed at Pentecost. 'We only live, only surprise, consumed by either fire or fire,' acknowledged T.S. Eliot. Those in the Christian tradition who have prayed for the 'pure, celestial fire', to be kindled in their hearts are well aware that an invisible, untouchable flame is one of God's greatest gifts.

6 Outside the camp   *Read Hebrews 13:9–25*

No abiding city The Church of the Holy Sepulchre in Jerusalem can disappoint its visitors in a number of ways. Not least in the fact that it is now situated firmly within the old walled city of Jerusalem. It is of small comfort to our imaginations to be told that in the time of Christ the city wall lay to the south of its present line, and the site of the church was probably a quarry outside the city. The place simply does not fit the bill of a green hill without a city wall! Yet though Mrs Alexander's hymn may be guilty of a certain romanticism, it is true to an important New Testament insight. For the author of Hebrews the fact that Christ was crucified *outside* the city is not just a statement of geography but leads to an important theological insight. In this last chapter the 'cultic' language which has loomed large earlier in the epistle is recapitulated, but is now applied in ways that are more human and humane. So the geography of Christ's death fits his role of the scapegoat whose sacrificial blood was carried outside the camp of Israel (Leviticus 16:20–28). Yet it also bears implications for Christ's followers that are removed from any cultic sphere. They too must remain outside the camp, identifying with those whom society casts off. And since 'the camp' concerned was originally the camp of Israel, the author seems to be asking his readers to move beyond the traditional boundaries of Judaism. It could be a dangerous place to be.

Stephen found it so as he spoke of a God who could not travel outside man-made camps or tents or temples. No accident then that Stephen, the disciple who mirrored Christ so closely, was himself cast outside the city before he was stoned.

Great shepherd of the sheep But for most of us, most of the time, the sacrifice demanded in response to Christ's own is of a different order, and for that we must be grateful. Echoes appear in these final verses to suggest that our sacrifice includes the praise of God—on our lips and in our lives (v. 15)—and the prayer that in doing his will we can 'please' him as it was once believed in the Old Testament sacrifices did (v. 21). The magnificent blessing which includes this prayer and with which the epistle draws to its close recalls the equally impressive way in which the letter had opened. The same themes are there: glory, sacrifice, victory over death. The difference is that we have moved from a world of angels to humans and even to sheep. We may have no abiding city, Christ may be leading us like a nomadic shepherd across an open wilderness: but a shepherd must and will, touch, cherish and intimately care for his flock.

GUIDELINES

'The life of humanity is the vision of God.' The readings this week perhaps lead our thoughts to the second half of that quotation from St Irenaeus (see page 104). Hebrews has affirmed our worth as human beings: now the epistle tells us that if our vision is restricted to earthly and material parameters we will not discover the full privilege and responsibility that comes with being sons and daughters of God. The quest for the vision of God is never a comfortable quest, not least because our God is not always a comfortable God (12:29). We may need to journey as Abraham and our ancestors in the faith did before us. We may find that in our journey to the heavenly Jerusalem we must reject, or are rejected by, the earthly Jerusalems or cities we inhabit.

But will we not discover, as Stephen did, that the glory of God is now no longer to be seen in earthly temples and structures, but outside the camp and beyond the city wall?

Jesus and Prayer

One of the great themes of the letter to the Hebrews is the high priesthood of Jesus Christ. The letter maintains that heaven and earth are linked, not by a temporal priesthood operating in an earthly sanctuary, but by one whose experience took him from earth to heaven through the suffering that culminated in execution. Those who place their confidence in the sacrifice of the high priest Jesus can expect to enjoy the immediacy of fellowship with God, and the benefits this brings to human life.

These ideas are rooted in Jesus' own teaching about prayer, as this short series of readings from the Gospels demonstrates. Jesus encourages his disciples to believe that his way of praying will unite heaven and earth, by bringing the benefits of God's kingdom to bear on earth. Prayer is a vital weapon in God's way of redeeming the world, but only if we pray diligently and humbly. The Gospel accounts of Jesus' prayer can act as resources for our prayer, not least in the way they draw us into his concerns for his disciples, the Church and the world.

The notes are based on the New Revised Standard Version, but they can be used with any modern translation.

---

28 JULY–3 AUGUST

---

1 Confident prayer   Read Luke 11:1–13

Luke is fond of showing Jesus at prayer, and his practice has obviously impressed the disciple who asks, 'Lord, teach us to pray'. What was it about Jesus' prayer life that made such an impact on his followers? Luke's distillation of the essence of Jesus' teaching about prayer may provide the answer.

Jesus begins by giving his disciples a simple prayer (vv. 2–4), starting with his favourite name for God, *Abba* ('daddy'—much more affectionate and intimate than our rather formal 'father'). Then he goes on to tell a story which encourages his disciples to be confident whenever they ask for God's help (vv. 5–8). Finally, he returns to the *Abba* imagery to underline the ground of this confidence: even more than a human father, the heavenly *Abba* knows what his children need, and is more than willing to provide it (vv. 9–11).

The disciples may well have been impressed by the intimacy and immediacy of Jesus' prayer. What does this enable him to say about prayer?

First, *keep prayer simple*. The prayer Jesus gave is easily remembered (it is a trimmed-down version of our 'Lord's Prayer'). Its language is direct, and rooted in everyday experience. Its theme is the straightforward request that God's reliable and dependable strength might prevail in the world ('your kingdom come'), so that we might have what we need and no more ('give us each day our daily bread'). Jesus' prayer expects compassion to be the order of the day ('forgive us our sins, as we ourselves forgive...'), and asks for strength to stand firm when faith is tested ('do not bring us to the time of trial'). In its direct address to God, its accessible language and its concern with everyday life, Jesus' prayer is essentially *simple*.

Jesus' second point is *don't be afraid to ask for God's help*. In Jesus' world, village hospitality could always be taken for granted. Even if you knocked up your neighbour in the middle of the night, you could count on his help—to withhold it from someone in need would only bring down shame on the whole household. The conventions of Palestinian hospitality would ensure that neighbours and friends got what they needed. So those who pray can be confident that God will help them whenever they ask.

Jesus' third point outlines the form God's help takes: *don't underestimate God's sympathy and generosity*. For all their failings, human fathers are sufficiently considerate and kind to give their hungry children what they need. How much more does God satisfy the deepest needs of his children, by giving the Holy Spirit—his life-giving presence and energy—to those who go on asking. Persevering in prayer brings its own rewards.

Jesus teaches his disciples to be confident in prayer. When they—and we—pray simply, directly and diligently, the heavenly *Abba* is never less than generous with himself.

2 Pray like this   *Read Matthew 6:7–15*

Matthew's version of the Lord's Prayer has a different context from Luke's. Here there is no request that Jesus teach his disciples to pray. Instead Jesus suggests a style of praying utterly at odds with Gentile wordiness. There is no need to offer prayers that are so long and detailed that God is left in no doubt as to what the petitioner wants. Prayer should be brief and to the point, wholly taken up with the glory of God rather than human needs and desires.

The theme of the Lord's Prayer is the union of heaven and earth. Elaborate and carefully-orchestrated religious ritual is unnecessary—the invocation of God as *Abba* is enough. By using Jesus' preferred name for God, the one who prays enters into the beloved Son's relationship with his heavenly Father (see Matthew 3:17). This suggests that prayer is not simply a form of words, but a way of expressing the deep desire to share in the mission of Jesus.

There is only one basic request in Jesus' preferred way of praying: 'your kingdom come'—that is, 'let the heavenly order of righteousness appear in the world; let earthly life be ruled by heaven's ways'. Bread symbolizes the needs of the unredeemed world. 'Daily bread' is better translated as 'bread for the coming day', when God's kingdom arrives. 'Let earth be so ruled by heaven that God's children have whatever they need.'

In a hostile and deeply divided world, one of the most obvious needs is mercy. Mercy is one of the hallmarks of God's blessing and reign (Matthew 5:7); it is the 'daily bread' that nourishes reconciliation and peace. The request for forgiveness seeks to realize heaven's essential mercy in earth's affairs. Verses 14 and 15 come as a footnote to verse 12. How can earth receive heaven's generosity, if the two are moving in opposite directions? If we refuse to forgive, we perpetuate the cycles of violence in our dealings with one another.

It is often the experience of those who pray that their requests are frustrated—heaven does not appear on earth at a stroke. Prayer is part of the struggle for redemption. As faith is tested in the face of conflict, loyalty to God's kingdom can be undermined. Hence the request to be delivered from the time of trial and rescued from the evil one. Nothing must be allowed to get in the way of the arrival of God's reign.

Busy people will be encouraged by Jesus' recommendation to keep their prayers brief and to the point. But such prayer will only nourish the rich variety of work we do for the coming of God's kingdom if it avoids superficiality. Brevity must not be traded in for depth.

3 Prayer as a weapon *Read Mark 9:14–29*

In the absence of Jesus, the faith of nine of his disciples failed the test and their prayer withered and died. This is the conclusion we can draw from Jesus' words in verse 29. He and the inner circle of disciples—Peter, James and John—had been away on the mountain, where their sublime experience of heaven on earth contrasted sharply with the remaining disciples' ridiculous plight. They had evidently failed to help the spirit-possessed child (in Matthew 17:15 he is described as 'epileptic') who had been brought to them, despite being given authority to do so (Mark 6:7).

His father is desperate by the time Jesus arrives on the scene. He hopes that Jesus can help his son, but he is aware that his faith is not all that it might be. However, what counts is that *Jesus'* faith is sufficient to rid the boy of the destructive powers that have held him since childhood. The nine disciples had not even had enough faith to pray over the lad!

Jesus emphasizes the importance of prayer in the struggle against the destructive forces that oppose the God of life. This suggests that he sees prayer as a weapon—God fights his battles through prayer. Is this how we see Christian prayer? Many popular forms of prayer—not all of them Christian, or even religious—associate it with stillness rather than struggle. And some contemporary versions of meditation seem to be nothing more than acquiring a positive mental outlook. Do these forms of prayer and meditation have anything in common with Jesus' understanding of prayer as a weapon?

The prayer of stillness helps people become more 'focused', more 'centred', more in touch with their inner selves. Jesus certainly saw prayer as a way of becoming more centred—not on ourselves, though, but on God and his reign of justice and compassion. Jesus certainly believed that prayer has a positive power for good—not as a form of positive thinking, though, but as a way of focusing on the goodness and love of God which redeems the world. Jesus' own faith enabled him to be so open to God's justice and compassion, goodness and love that *his* prayer was the decisive weapon in God's redeeming purposes.

Even when faith falls short of all that it might be, it can still act as a channel of God's justice and compassion, goodness and love. Our prayer might not heal all the world's ills, but it can certainly be a weapon in the struggle to make the world a better place. As you think about your own prayers, can you work out how this might be true for you?

4 Persistence and humility in prayer *Read Luke 18:1–14*

These two parables are linked by the theme of vindication—the expectation that God will stand by those who have the courage to pray in faith. What are the essential characteristics of such faith, and its prayer?

The first parable depends on the 'how much more' comparison found in the story we read earlier from Luke 11:5–8: if something is true of human beings, *how much more* is it true of God. Presumably the widow had no-one else to stand up for her interests: the judge was her last hope in the struggle for justice. For his part, he felt no moral obligation, either to God or the people over whose lives he had such power. But eventually the widow's persistence prevailed, and the judge—acting purely out of self-interest—vindicated her. The widow represents destitute members of society, whose trials are only compounded by their dealings with indifferent and hard-hearted officials who care nothing for justice. If a judge like this can be persuaded to act favourably, *how much more* will God come to the help of those who persevere in prayer. According to Jesus, God stands by those whose prayer is carried on a wave of persistence.

If the hero of the first parable is economically destitute, the hero in the second is a social and religious outcast. Jesus' answer in verse 14 would have shocked the parable's first hearers and readers, who would have expected the Pharisee to be honoured by God. He and his kind take their obligations to God and Israel seriously, unlike the tax-collector, who makes his living by collaborating with Gentiles and cheating his own people. But for all his respectability and conventional piety, the Pharisee is at a disadvantage. Rich in moral rectitude, almsgiving and fasting he may be; but he is poor when it comes to humility. The tax-collector takes the contempt the public feel for him into the place of prayer. His social shame encourages him to be humble before God, whereas the Pharisee confuses popular respect with divine approval, and presumes far too much of God. According to Jesus, God stands by those whose prayer is carried on a wave of humility.

The destitute and the outcast may have to struggle to gain a hearing from their powerful and respectable contemporaries, but not from God—nor, hopefully, from those who pray for the coming of God's kingdom.

5 Prayer and integrity *Read Mark 14:32–42*

As Jesus sought to encourage his disciples to stand firm in the trials and tribulations that lay ahead of them, he called on them to be alert and awake—like servants given the responsibility of looking after their master's interests while he is away (Mark 13:32–37). At the last supper, he warned them that what was about to happen to him would not leave them unscathed: they would be like sheep distressed by the removal of their trusted shepherd (14:46–31). In Gethsemane, Jesus is no more than a few metres away from his disciples. Yet it is evident that his earlier words have fallen on deaf ears. Instead of being alert to what is happening to Jesus, and staying awake to support him in prayer, they succumb to the power of sleep. While he is all but overcome by grief and anxiety, they allow their tiredness to get the better of them.

There are echoes of Jesus' teaching about prayer in the words he addresses both to God and his sleeping disciples. God is still *Abba*, even when he asks his beloved Son to drink the cup of suffering. The Father's reliable and dependable strength might still prevail by delivering Jesus from the violence that awaits him. But Jesus is prepared to abandon any ideas of self-preservation at this stage, in favour of 'your will be done'. The disciples—whose representative, Peter, had earlier declared his willingness to suffer with Jesus rather than deny him (14:31)—are about to face their time of trial, which will severely test their loyalty to Jesus and his cause. What is tragic is that they hardly appear to be alert to what is happening around them.

In Gethsemane, Jesus once again demonstrates his integrity: he lives as he prays, and prays as he lives. He does not deny for a moment the depth of his agony, or the challenge it presents to his desire to obey the One he calls *Abba*. But he holds on to his trust in the good purposes of God, whose Son and servant he is. Christian prayer can rely on the integrity of Jesus. When we fall well short of his example and teaching, he remains alert to his responsibilities to those whom he calls to follow him (see vv. 27–28).

In Luke's account of the last supper, Jesus tells Peter of his prayer for him as he and the other disciples face the unsettling attention of Satan (Luke 22:32). John—whose narrative often overlaps with Luke's—provides a much longer account of Jesus' prayer for his disciples as he prepares to leave them in death. As in Jesus' Gethsemane prayer (which John leaves out), there are elements here which remind us of the Lord's Prayer, as well as some distinctively Johannine themes.

The prayer is addressed to God as *Abba*, and its chief concern is that God should be honoured in all that is about to happen. Jesus obviously has in mind his imminent glorification through his passion. But he also looks ahead to the enjoyment of eternal life by the community of disciples which his mission has brought into being (vv. 3–5). If the Lord's Prayer looks for the union of heaven and earth ('your kingdom come, your will be done, on earth as it is in heaven'), here Jesus prays that the essential features of his own relationship with *Abba* should continue to be reflected in his followers. They already recognize the truth of his heavenly origin and authority (vv. 7–8). But they live in a hostile world, which imperils their unity and loyalty to Jesus' teaching (vv. 11, 14, 21–23). As they embark on their mission, they will need to reckon with the power of evil that assaulted Jesus throughout his ministry. So Jesus prays that his own joyful dedication to God—expressed supremely in the self-sacrifice that returns him to the heavenly realm—will be reproduced in them (vv. 13–19).

Heaven and earth meet in the coming of Jesus, and by extension in the common life of his followers. This is why the unity of the Church is so important. The world will believe in the essential truth of Jesus—that he is sent by God as the expression of divine love for the world (v. 21; cf. John 3:16)—if his followers are also seen to be the dwelling place of God's glory and love (vv. 22–24, 26; cf. John 1:14), and if the Son's knowledge of the Father is found in them (v. 25). The disunity of the Church is nothing less than a scandal (the Greek root of this word means 'stumbling block').

This last prayer of Jesus before his passion is also his continuing prayer for his Church—the everlasting concern of the risen Christ that his followers should keep faith with all that he has revealed to them. Truly Christian prayer, offered in the name of Jesus (John 14:13f), enters into the prayer of the heavenly Christ, and allows itself to be drawn into his concerns for the Church and the world. What might be the fruits of this prayer in you and your church?

GUIDELINES

This week's readings have shown how fundamental the Lord's Prayer is for our understanding of Jesus' teaching about, and practice of, prayer. Read through the Lord's Prayer slowly, and ask yourself the following questions:

• *How far do I share the basic attitude of Jesus, that I can address God with confidence as the heavenly Abba who will always respond generously and sympathetically to my needs?*

• *How much is this simple and direct prayer a model for my own prayers?*

• *How far is my prayer part of my struggle to promote the values of God's kingdom at home, in my church and neighbourhood, in my places of work and leisure?*

• *Can I honestly say that my prayer is characterized by perseverance and humility?*

• *What evidence is there of my attempts to live as I pray and pray as I live?*

• *How much is my prayer taken up with my own anxieties and preoccupations, and how far does it help to draw me into Jesus' concerns for the Church and the world?*

1 Samuel 1–16

The first verse of the old Sunday School hymn, 'God has given us a book full of stories' ends,

It begins with the tale of a garden
and ends with the city of gold.

The second begins, 'But the best is the story of Jesus...' and best implies that there are other Bible stories which are not so good. Some of those in 1 Samuel 1–16 come into this category. Here is a collection of ancient tales, adding up to a sad and not very edifying story.

Whenever and wherever these stories were first told they appear where they do in the Hebrew Bible as part of a longer tragedy. The books of Joshua, Judges, Samuel and Kings tell the story of the people of Israel from a bright beginning on the wrong side of the Jordan River into, and then out of the Promised Land, and away to exile in Babylon. This tragic story is followed by four explanations (Isaiah, Jeremiah, Ezekiel and The Twelve) which repeat the same message—the people of Israel are the people of God and the tragedy is that their misfortune is of their own making. The theme of the story and the message of the explanation is the same—they have brought the catastrophe of the exile upon themselves by their disobedience and wrongdoing.

Occasionally this message is made explicit, as when Samuel says to the people, 'If you will fear the Lord and serve him and heed his voice and not rebel against the commandment of the Lord, and if both you and the king who reigns over you will follow the Lord your God, it will be well; but if you will not heed the voice of the Lord, but rebel against the commandment of the Lord, then the hand of the Lord will be against you and your king' (1 Samuel 12:14–15).

Mostly it lies hidden in the story itself. And no doubt this story wasn't told and retold simply as a history lesson. It had a moral for the present and the future of the people of God. So the message of 1 Samuel 1–16 is this, heard early on in Hannah's Song:

He will guard the feet of his faithful ones,
but the wicked shall be cut off in darkness;
for not by might does one prevail.

1 Samuel 2:9

But the plot is much more subtle, for who are the 'faithful ones' and who the 'wicked'? Hannah sings of risings and fallings, but in the story each rise leads to a fall and there are no heroes. Neither Samuel nor Saul come out of it very well. It is a story of fathers and sons. Eli's bad sons bring about Samuel's rise, but his sons turn out no better than Eli's and Saul's good son cannot prevent his father's fall. At the end we come to David, the true anointed one, in whose story the same themes of risings and fallings and fathers and sons will continue. In all its characters the story teases us with the ambiguities of human success and failure.

The version used is the New Revised Standard Version (NRSV). Bibles with footnotes will make it clear that in these chapters the traditional Hebrew text often varies considerably from the ancient translations and from a Hebrew text recently discovered among the Dead Sea Scrolls found at Qumran.

4–10 AUGUST   1 SAMUEL 1:1—3:18

1   The scene is set   *Read 1 Samuel 1:1–18*

First we meet a man with a childless wife. Here are echoes of Abraham and Sarah (Genesis 16–17), Rebekah (Genesis 25:21) and especially Rachel, childless and taunted by her husband's other wife (Genesis 30:1). The story of Samson begins with exactly the same words as this one (Judges 13:2). All these are stories of God doing something special. So a mood begins to be created.

In the first scene are Elkanah, Hannah and Peninnah—and God. A family from another culture and another age, but not a happy family. Here, as often in Bible stories, the on-stage actors only know half of what is going on. Hannah knows she is childless, but only we readers know the cause (v. 5), and we wonder why God should be doing this. In the other stories he opens wombs. But there is humour too, as in the portrayal of Elkanah. For the life of him he can't see why Hannah should get so worked up about not having a son; after all, doesn't she have him? Verses 5 and 8 are unclear but that's the gist of them.

In the second scene we see Hannah and Eli. In distress Hannah prays and vows to give the son she prays for to God in a special way. Every firstborn male was dedicated to God: but in the case of

Hannah's son there would be an extra dedication. She would give him to the Lord for all of his life, and that would be a teetotal life without a razor! The NRSV uses the technical word here for such a consecrated person, Nazirite (see Numbers 6:5). Eli watches, apologizes, listens and blesses. Hannah leaves the matter with God, believes and goes in peace.

These opening verses set the scene and raise our expectations: a childless woman and an unsympathetic co-wife, a prayer out of deep affliction, a promise to God. We are invited to read on, wondering if God will answer Hannah, and if this is a significant story we are starting to read.

2 The gift is given   Read 1 Samuel 1:19–28

The gift is given (vv. 19–20). Returning home Elkanah makes love to Hannah ('Elkanah knew Hannah') and the Lord fulfils his plans for her ('the Lord remembered her'). Like most recent translations the NRSV perseveres in using Hebrew idioms for these two events, even at the risk of misleading us into thinking that God might forget something. So a son is born and named, the first of several namings in 1 Samuel. The boy is called 'Samuel', which Hannah explains as 'Asked of God', because that is how he came about. The scientific etymology of this name is rather different, which has led to theories which (unfortunately) divert attention from the story. The point of these two verses, incorrect etymology included, is to emphasize that the conception of this child is emphatically the Lord's work.

The vow is honoured (vv. 21–28). Elkanah's prayer that the Lord will 'establish his word' (v. 23) reads a little oddly at first, and some modern translations and ancient versions change 'his' to 'your', which certainly makes sense. But in so doing they miss a point, which is that all of these events are the work of God. Elkanah has seen this, and so he prays that as the child's conception was really the Lord's work, so may his total dedication be.

Hannah's offering, when it is finally given, is more than generous. Not only does she offer her firstborn son, but also a generous offering besides. The Hebrew text makes it more generous still, for in verse 24 Hannah takes three bulls up to Shiloh. Our modern translations follow the ancient Greek and Syriac and the manuscript from Qumran. Verses 27–28 contain a play on words which our translations cannot reproduce. 'Petition' and 'made' in verse 27 (literally 'the asking which I asked') are from the same verb as 'lent' and 'given' in verse 28 (I suppose there is even a connection between those four English words if you look hard enough). The facts that the three root letters of these words spell the name Saul, and that the etymology of 'Saul' really is 'Asked of God', is another reminder, if we needed one, that this story is no simple tale. But, as the hymn says, God is working his purpose out. So far, so good.

3 Hannah's Song *Read 1 Samuel 2:1–10*

Hannah's Song echoes through the Bible: in Mary's Song in Luke 1:46–55, in those Psalms which talk of a God who turns things upside down (e.g. 18:27; 75; 94; 113:7–9, compare Isaiah 2:7–19) and in those places where earthly values are stood on their head (e.g. in the Beatitudes in Matthew 5:1–12). In a real sense Jesus lives out Hannah's Song.

It is a feature of story-telling in the Old Testament to insert songs, poems or psalms at key points, as David's Song (which is Psalm 18) is inserted in 2 Samuel 22. Hannah's Song is one such psalm, though we have no other version of it anywhere else. It has all the features of a 'royal psalm' in the form of a thanksgiving spoken by, or on behalf of, the king. It links with Hannah's experience specifically in verse 5 and generally in its theme of God raising up the despised and bringing down the proud. It fits too as part of the longer story, with its final reference to God's 'king', his 'anointed' one (messiah) in verse 10. Messiah is simply the English form of the Hebrew word for Anointed One, which was what kings of Judah were called because they were anointed at their coronation.

Verse 10 sets the scene for much of what follows, for the stories of Samuel, Saul and David are stories about struggles for power. This verse insists that there is only one king-maker, the Lord, and that it is the Lord alone who gives strength to his king and exalts the power of his anointed. But who is his king? And who is his anointed? For the story which follows is not only of the failure of the first anointed king, Saul, and the beginnings of the reign of David, but the longer story of the failure of David's monarchy too! The importance of this song in the context of the exile is clear. The exile is God's punishment on the proud and any hope for the future lies in his raising those who are poor and broken.

4 False sons and a true *Read 1 Samuel 2:11–26*

This is a section of contrast, but before we trace it look at what is missing from verse 11. There is no mention of Hannah, or her feelings, at all!

The contrast is made by alternating glimpses of the goodness of Samuel (vv. 11, 18–21, 26) with longer scenes of the badness of Eli's sons (vv. 12–17, 22–25). Elkanah leaves and Samuel remains to minister to the Lord. He is now old enough to act in the story. He does what he should, watched by Eli, and everyone approves of him—Eli, the people and God. Behind his back Eli's sons do not behave as priests should, and even their bad behaviour is inconsistent, do they want boiled meat or not (vv. 13–15)? The people are horrified by their behaviour, as is Eli when they tell him, and so is God. They refuse to listen to Eli, but what are we to make of the last sentence of verse 25? The story simply says that this is all part of the Lord's overall plan, the same Lord who before had 'hardened Pharaoh's heart' (Exodus 7:3, etc) and later will send an evil spirit into Saul (1 Samuel 16:14). Some commentators explain this by saying that here Hebrew identifies cause with effect, and that may be true: but it is perhaps better simply to recognize that the storyteller is not a twentieth-century Christian.

Samuel is growing into a true son for Eli and a faithful priest to God, though he is neither natural son nor of priestly line. Those who are the sons of Eli and of priestly descent are no proper sons or priests at all.

5 God against Eli *Read 1 Samuel 2:27–36*

Here is the first significant bit-part in the story. An unnamed 'man of God' (that is, a prophet, someone who speaks for God) comes to Eli and his opening words, 'Thus says the Lord' are traditional ones which confirm that he brings a message from God.

The message is devastatingly simple. He announces the replacement of Eli and his family as priests. Tracing priestly lines in the Old Testament is highly complicated, and the reality was no doubt more complex still, but here the point is simple. God can change his mind if things don't work out as he intends. They haven't. So he will.

Verse 28 is a neat nutshell description of a priest's duties. The ephod mentioned here is not the simple priestly robe of verse 19: but either (as in Exodus 28:5–35) the elaborate garment which contained a pocket for the Urim and Thummim, stones by which the priest could cast lots to ascertain God's will, or (as in 1 Samuel 14:3, 23:6, 9 and 30:7) some sort of box or pouch for carrying them.

Running through this message is a deliberate confusion—Eli and his house are confused with the whole house of Israel—as the prophet looks both backwards and forwards. Looking backwards, who is this 'ancestor' in verse 27, is it Aaron, the official ancestor of the priests, or Moses, the ancestor of all the people? Looking forwards, the fate of whoever is meant in verse 33 is very close to that of King Zedekiah in the exile in 2 Kings 25:1–7. So whose wrongdoing and punishment is announced here, Eli's and his family or Israel's? The good news in verse 35 picks up the promise of 2:10, but is this new future about Samuel as God's faithful priest, or a new king to come after the exile? The message is deliberately vague: but its allusions and implications, bad and good, for those of the exiled generation would be clear.

6 'Samuel! Samuel!' *Read 1 Samuel 3:1–18*

Those who went to Sunday School will remember this as a favourite lesson. Others might be familiar with the Victorian hymn, 'Hushed was the evening hymn', which is still a helpful meditation on the passage. The story itself is simple and touching and needs little comment.

At first sight verse 1 seems odd. We have only just read a 'word of the Lord' from the unnamed prophet. Perhaps this shows one of the joins where two stories were put together, but as it is it serves to reinforce God's total rejection of Eli and his line. If God's word was rare, then for the same person to receive the same message twice it must be important.

The ark of God appears for the first time in verse 3. It features large in later stories and we will look at its significance then.

For me the central character in this story is Eli rather than Samuel. I read of the faithful listening ear of the old man, who encourages Samuel to listen to the voice and then insists that he tell what it says, even though he knows what he will hear will destroy him. Then in verse 18b he responds, not with resignation, but with the sort of trustful obedience that is the mark of faithfulness in many Old Testament stories, seen at its highest in the Authorized Version translation of Job 13:15, 'Though he slay me, yet will I trust in him.'

An obvious question is, why read an ancient story like this? One answer is—because it's a true account of the events it portrays. But if it isn't, and it is very difficult for us to believe that it is when it tells, for example, of God opening and closing a womb, then that answer falls flat. Another answer might be that like all good stories it has important things to say about God and the meaning of life, the universe and everything. And we have already seen that it is a good story with an intriguing plot and real characters. There are obvious dangers in turning stories into doctrines or in hardening poetry into prose; and Jesus' use of parables encourages us to read a story like 1 Samuel with our eyes open. It is as if those who included this book in our Bibles are saying to us, 'If you have eyes to see, then see!'

11–17 AUGUST   **1 SAMUEL 3:19—8:22**

---

1 A capture and many deaths   *Read 1 Samuel 3:19—4:11*

In verses 19–21 the story-teller moves us quickly down the years. Samuel fulfills his early promise. He is now a national figure, known from far north (Dan) to deep south (Beersheba). His credentials are superb—he is a prophet to whom the Lord appears regularly (unlike in the old days of v. 1) and gives messages. But we will hear nothing more of Samuel for twenty years (until 7:3).

Chapters 4:1b—7:2 tell a new story about the ark. The disaster which has been lurking since God's messages to Eli now strikes. The Philistines, unheard of since Samson's time (Judges 16:30), reappear. They were a Mediterranean people (part of the Sea Peoples, as the Egyptians called them) expanding eastwards, arriving in the west of Palestine and settling on the coastal plain just as Israel was emerging in the central highlands. And contrary to our use of the adjective 'philistine', they appear to have been both cultured and technologically advanced. They are major actors in the unfolding drama.

After their initial defeat the Israelites resort to Plan B, bringing the 'ark of the covenant of the Lord' from Shiloh to the battlefield. This is a holy war. With the ark, the Lord himself takes to the field (v. 3). The

Good News Bible calls the ark the 'Covenant Box', an accurate if not very elegant description of this most sacred object. It was a portable shrine or chest, later said to contain the tablets of the Ten Commandments, symbolizing the presence and power of the Lord (Exodus 25:10–22; Deuteronomy 10:1–5). It was seen as God's throne or footstool with cherubim (winged sphinxes?) standing guard over it and God 'enthroned' on or above them (v. 4). Note the association of the ark with the name of God as 'Lord of hosts.' This is an old title which honours God either as the Lord of the Israelite armies, or, more likely, as the king of the heavenly hosts, which may be the heavenly beings which surround his throne or the stars. Much better to leave the possibilities open than to translate it as 'the Lord Almighty' as is sometimes done.

The Philistines refuse to give in to their real fear (vv. 6–9). They fight. They win.

2 'Ichabod' *Read 1 Samuel 4:12–22*

The news of defeat is brought to the aged and infirm Eli. He hears the news of his sons unmoved. The news about the ark kills him.

His obituary is brief, 'He had judged Israel forty years' (v. 18b). He will be the last but one judge (that is, leader, chieftain). Some commentators point out that Eli has little in common with the charismatic leaders of previous groups or generations after whom the book of Judges is named, and that is so. But then neither has Samuel who takes up this task after him (1 Samuel 7:6), because our story is a story of transition. We are moving towards the time when it is a king who will, rightly or wrongly, well or badly, exercise this role of being the saviour and deliverer of God's people (1 Samuel 8:5; 1 Kings 3:9 where NRSV has 'govern').

The chapter ends with another birth and naming, but one very different from the last. Before she dies the nameless mother gives her son the desolate name, 'Ichabod', and the meaning of the name, 'The glory has departed from Israel' is given twice. We are left in no doubt of the desolation it implies. Here again an incorrect etymology adds to the meanings of the story. 'Ichabod' probably means 'No-glory' or 'Where is the glory?', but the mother gives it a much stronger meaning. It is, 'The glory has departed' or better 'The glory is exiled', words full of meaning for all later readers.

For the mother the name signifies the tragic loss of the ark and the deaths of her father-in-law and husband. But the story-teller doesn't tell it like that. Their death is not loss but a long-planned gain. We have known that it was coming since 2:12. And although we have not been prepared in the same way for the loss of the ark, our reaction to its loss is less than hers. We feel that it has not been lost by the bravery of the Philistines, but by the will of the one who is enthroned on it. We are learning that Israel cannot manipulate or control God, not even by using his most sacred symbols. What matters is obedience. Nothing else. It is a hard lesson.

3 A terror to its captors *Read 1 Samuel 5*

Now it is the Philistines who learn that it is the ark, and the Lord enthroned upon it, which is in control. In verses 1–2 they carry 'the ark of God' hither and yon at will, just as the Israelites had. Their lesson begins in verse 3. They begin to discover that they have a trophy, 'the ark of the Lord', they could do without. The ark is mentioned thirty-six times in these chapters, referred to mainly as the ark of the Lord, the ark of God, and the ark of the God of Israel. Notice where the different titles are used and who uses them.

The Philistines controlled the coastal plain from what we call the Gaza Strip north for thirty miles and east for twenty with their five cities of Gaza, Gath, Ashkelon, Ashdod and Ekron. Dagon was an old Canaanite god—in their pantheon he was the father of Baal—adopted by the Philistines as their main deity. There was possibly a temple to him in each city, though only the ones at Ashdod and Gaza (Judges 16:23) are mentioned in the Bible.

In the Ashdod temple Dagon was represented by a statue in human form, and the first disaster the ark causes is to that statue. Dagon prostrates himself in worship before the ark of the Lord! Whether this is satirical, ironic, humorous or serious each reader has to judge. Verse 5 is an example of a reference to the origin of a custom or saying which we find from time to time in Old Testament story-telling (e.g. Genesis 22:14; 32:32; Joshua 4:9), though what this particular custom was is hard to say. Then disaster strikes the city, and each city to which in desperation they move the ark. In verse 6 the Hebrew text mentions a plague of 'tumours', and the Greek adds one of mice, which appear in the Hebrew in the next chapter. This suggests that the writer has bubonic plague in mind. The Authorized Version and the New Jewish Publication Society translation have haemorrhoids rather than 'tumours'. In 6:4 the idea of gold images of plague tumours is bad enough, but images of piles...

4   Getting rid of it   *Read 1 Samuel 6:1—7:1*

In verses 1–2 we see that the Philistines have recognized what the ark really is, that it is the ark of the Lord, and so they wish to return it to its proper place with due reverence to him. The religious experts advise sending a 'guilt offering' with the ark when it is returned. In this way they will be healed, 'ransomed' (NRSV is following the Greek and the Qumran Hebrew manuscript here) and left alone. There may be hints here of the 'spoiling of the Egyptians' (Exodus 3:21) for the exodus stories are referred to explicitly in verse 6, or simply of the principle that God should not be approached empty-handedly either when thanking him or seeking something from him (Exodus 23:15; Deuteronomy 16:16–17). To give their gold in the forms of tumours and mice reflects belief in the same sort of symbolism that prompted Moses to hold up a bronze snake to save the people from snakebite (Numbers 21:9).

In verses 8–12 we see the same sort of test as Gideon putting out his fleece (Judges 6:37–40) or Elijah covering his altar with water (1 Kings 18:33–35). If cows which have never been hitched to a cart and which have only just been separated from their calves keep going away from them it must be God at work. Note the last part of verse 9 and what it says about 'chance'.

The ark is welcomed back to Israel by the folk of Beth-shemesh and the Levites offer appropriate sacrifices (vv. 13–15). The Levites, seen elsewhere as the proper guardians of the ark, appear only three times in Samuel and Kings. Suffice to say that they are another branch of the priesthood which complicates the already complex picture, both in the Old Testament and beyond it.

6:19—7:1 looks like a fragment of an older and primitive story, but the meaning is clear. The Lord's holiness is not to be trifled with (see also the other story of the ark in 2 Samuel 6:6–8). The details are difficult even though our English translations follow the Greek in removing the worst textual problems (the Hebrew text suggests 50,070 victims!). We do not know who Jeconiah was, nor what his descendants did to deserve what they got.

5 'Ebenezer' *Read 1 Samuel 7:2–17*

Here is a cycle of blessing–disobedience–misery–repentance–deliverance–blessing and the role of God and his 'judge' in it all reminiscent of the book of Judges.

If verse 1 reflects the blessing, verse 2 hints at the misery. Contrary to what we might have expected after 3:19—4:1a and 7:1, the next twenty years were not good. The expression 'lamented after the Lord' (NRSV) is a very literal translation of the Hebrew. The sad state of affairs is confirmed in Samuel's speech which follows.

Samuel reappears in verse 3 and calls the people to repent. Though the ark had returned safely, the people have not been loyal to the Lord. As often in Judges this speech cites worshipping 'foreign gods' as the main symptom of disobedience. From exodus to exile the story is of Israel's repeated apostasy from its one true God, the Lord: but the story oversimplifies the realities. Even as late as the exile, belief in the Lord alone was only one of the theologies in ancient Israel. See for example Jeremiah 44:15–19, where worshippers of the Queen of Heaven argue with Jeremiah about who is the real heretic responsible for the fall of Jerusalem. Is it those who have turned against the Lord, as Jeremiah said, or those who have neglected the Queen of Heaven, as the people said? Baal ('Lord' or 'Husband') was the main god of the Canaanites who appears frequently in apostasy stories and Astarte was his consort. The 'Baals' and 'Astartes' (Ashtaroth in some versions) are the local forms of these gods. These verses are full of irony: Dagon and the Philistines had acknowledged the Lord; not so his own people.

So Samuel invites all Israel to the sanctuary at Mizpah, where they perform some sort of ceremony involving water, fasting and confession. 'Saved' or 'delivered' is a better translation of the verb in the last sentence of verse 6, and in verses 7–11 that deliverance is completed by God. In a passage typical of Judges, the Philistine enemies are routed by God rather than by anything the Israelite fighters do. Even Samuel plays no military role. Then in verses 12–14 we have another naming, of the Ebenezer ('Stone of Help') memorial stone.

The chapter ends with blessing. Samuel is an honoured leader, but the picture of him as 'Judge' is moving away from the old style military leaders and towards that of a 'circuit judge'. He has, however, considerable power, because in addition to being 'judge' he is prophet and priest.

136

6 They want a king *Read 1 Samuel 8:1–22*

Samuel's sons turn out as badly as Eli's. So the elders gather with a pivotal request—they want a king. Historians exploring the origins of the monarchy in ancient Israel find much conflicting material in chapters 8–12. If one thing is clear, it is that these chapters reflect what we read in much of the Old Testament, that the monarchy is seen as a mixed blessing, and that it evoked very mixed feelings. One extreme sees it as an unmitigated disaster—it was the failings of the monarchy which led to the catastrophe of exile! The other extreme saw the monarchy as the good old days—which would return when a new anointed king, God's Messiah, came to the throne. No doubt there were views everywhere in between.

Samuel, reflecting the views of many of the prophets and of the editors responsible for the story from Joshua–2 Kings, is deeply suspicious of the whole enterprise. The story-teller will have had no trouble in collecting the material for Samuel's speech in verses 10–18.

This chapter is a watershed in the books of Joshua–2 Kings. The old ways are shown to have failed, and not even the most fervent anti-monarchist could say that all had been well in the days before they had kings. The question is, will the new ways fare any better? Samuel begs leave to doubt that they will. And they don't. Verses 7–8 suggest that the only way to keep all things right is to have God as king: but surely it is as impossible to ask that of a nation as it is to expect priests like Eli, charismatic leaders like Samuel, or anointed kings to rule as God requires?

GUIDELINES

These stories are set around 1075–1025BC and the story-teller has got the background history and geography right, as any good story-teller would. I have not commented on any of the dates or places mentioned in the stories, nor on the logistics of the battles. Some commentaries focus on precisely those things. Others ignore them, as I have, except where clarifying them helps to follow the story. My reasoning is that 1 Samuel is not a book about ancient history but about God. But avoiding one set of problems only leads us into another.

In these stories God acts. He closes and opens wombs, causes plagues and fights battles. Are we to read these stories literally and conclude that God acts in today's world? Some Christians have no problem in answering Yes, and saying that he cures the sick, finds you a car-parking space in a crowded city centre or protects your church from war-time bombs. Others, and I am one, have real problems with a God who intervenes, mainly because so often he doesn't! All this raises acute questions, for example, about what we are doing when we say prayers of petition or intercession.

Another difficulty this raises is with the idea of God's providence, that he has a plan for us. There are no problems with this idea at a very general level (God wants to bless us, God wanted me to be a Methodist Minister, etc) but it becomes more and more problematic the more specific you get. There are not many references in the Bible to things happening 'by chance', and 1 Samuel 6:9 is one of them. If there were more, perhaps Christians might be more ready to say, 'It was an accident' or 'It's just one of those things' when faced by some of the terrible, or the nice, chances and changes of life. These are difficult questions which the Bible compels us to think about.

I had a conversation recently with someone who said that he found it very uncomfortable to believe that God was not in control of his life. It was like being in a boat without a rudder. I said that it didn't feel like that to me, and I quoted two texts which are precious to me. The first was the hymn, 'In heavenly love abiding, no change my heart shall fear' (I could have added the other one, 'O love that wilt not let me go'). These hymns speak of us being held, no matter what, in God's love. The second was the old translation of Deuteronomy 33:27, 'The eternal God is thy refuge, and underneath are the everlasting arms.' Knowing that I am held in the love of God helps me to live without believing that God plans every detail of my life. It also helps me to pray for others, that they too may know what it is to be held in those arms, and also that I and others may be used by God as extra arms for those in need.

AUGUST 18–24   1 SAMUEL 9–13

1   **Saul arrives**   *Read 1 Samuel 9:1–21*

Verses 1–2, written in the same style as 1:1–2, begin a new chapter in the longer story. We know that the last chapter turned out very differently from what its opening sentences suggested (for its hero was the childless wife's son!); so what about this one? It seems that Saul has everything going for him, but will it turn out that way?

The story begins innocently enough with Saul, searching for straying donkeys, arriving at a strange town to ask the local holy man where they might be. The boy with him knows that he has a good reputation, but neither of them know his name. When the boy says, 'whatever he says comes true' (v. 6), we begin to realize that all this may not be as innocent as it looks, for we know what this 'man of God' has just said (in 8:11–18). In the Old Testament the new word 'prophet' (which replaced the older word 'seer', v. 9) covers everything from the national preacher to the local clairvoyant. The boy has enough to pay him for telling them what they want to know (does this boy remind you of another in a later story?).

Verses 11–15 emphasize Samuel's responsibilities at the shrine. He is the one who must bless the sacrifice and the people must wait for him to do it. Much will be made of this later in the story.

Unknown to Saul God has been at work and Samuel has been told what to do. He must anoint Saul as 'ruler' (never 'king' in 9:1—10:16, one of a number of signs in this chapter that we are reading a story made out of several older ones). The Lord's words in verse 16b echo those to Moses in Exodus 3:7.

Samuel's last sentence to Saul and Saul's reply can be read in many ways. Perhaps it is that the innocent Saul just doesn't understand and so responds respectfully and humbly to these strange words. Perhaps he is being evasive, as was Moses in Exodus 3:11. Or are Samuel's words ironic, or even sarcastic? Is Saul's modesty true or false? See also Gideon's reticence in Judges 6:15 and that of Jeremiah in 1:6.

2   The Lord's Anointed?   Read 1 Samuel 9:22—10:16

The bemused Saul is invited to the feast and eats as Samuel's honoured guest (vv. 22–24). He is given a special portion. The cut of the meat matters less than the fact that Saul is given it, unlike Eli's sons (even Samuel's?) who used to take what they wanted. Likewise after the meal Saul is given a place to sleep, rather than taking someone to sleep with.

Next day Samuel blesses Saul and the boy on their way, privately appoints him king by anointing him with olive oil (see also 1 Kings 1:39; 2 Kings 9:6) and tells him his God-given commission. Verse 1 is very short in the Hebrew, as the central part of the verse is missing, as the footnote in our Bibles indicates. This is a good example of how a scribe looks up, looks down again and continues copying, not noticing that he has started again at the same word later in the sentence. The meaning has been completed from the ancient Greek translation.

Samuel promises Saul three signs. The first will confirm Samuel's ability to see beyond the ordinary (v. 2). The second will confirm Saul's changed status (vv. 3–4). The one who had no bread to give to Samuel (9:7) is now given bread by those who are going to worship God. The third will confirm God's choice of Saul by filling him with God's power to do what is needed (vv. 5–7). Even so, verse 8 sounds a warning. It is Samuel who is still in control. The 'heart' in the Old Testament is the seat of the will rather than the emotions, so 'another heart' in verse 9 means a new will, courage, inner resolve, commitment.

The story only recounts the fulfilment of the third sign (vv. 10–13). Prophets working themselves into an ecstatic frenzy are a feature of many cultures, ancient and modern, and this group is yet another example of the variety of prophets and prophecy in the Old Testament. Verses 6 and 10 vividly express the power of the experience for Saul, but verses 12–13 seem ambivalent about it, or even sceptical. The un-named man's question sounds disdainful, and the meaning of the proverb is not clear. In 10:12 it seems to be used about disreputable behaviour on the part of somebody who ought to know better! These verses are difficult to explain, as is the sudden appearance of Saul's uncle and Saul's evasion of his question, with the curt answer, 'the donkeys had been found'.

3 The king is proclaimed Read 1 Samuel 10:17–27a

Samuel, as national leader, convenes an assembly; but this Samuel is not the one we last saw in chapter 8. They can have the king they crave, but he makes his objection clear. He speaks as a prophet using the classic 'Thus says the Lord' introduction. Note the key idea that they owe their life as a nation to the Lord who delivered them from slavery in Egypt and oppression from elsewhere and who now protects them. Whatever the actual origins of the various groups who eventually became the people of Israel, God's deliverance of the ancestors from Egypt became a key part of their folklore and the idea that they were a saved-against-the-odds nation of freed slaves was an important part of their national identity as well as of their faith. Thus the way God speaks in verse 18 (compare 8:8 and 12:7–8) is found in many other places, e.g. Exodus 20:2, Psalm 81:10, Jeremiah 11:4 and Micah 6:4.

Tribes, clans and families are not easily defined or described. The familiar twelve tribes of Israel is a later systematization of a rather more messy situation. In verse 22 the sort of clairvoyance used to find the lost asses is now needed to find Saul. We are left to imagine why he was hiding. God's secret choice and Samuel's secret anointing is confirmed by lot and acclamation.

Note the phrase about the 'rights and duties' of kingship in verse 25. The king in Israel is answerable to the Lord. When a later king, Josiah, reads a similar book discovered in the Jerusalem temple, he is brought up with a jolt and radical reforms follow (2 Kings 22:8–13). According to our story-teller most of the kings in between ignore both the Lord and their 'duties'.

The people go home. There is no doubt that God has blessed Saul. We see that in the comment about the 'warriors' who go with him, and in the fact that the only opposition to him now is from 'worthless men' (literally, 'sons of worthlessness (*belial*)', i.e. godless men, the same word as in 1:16 but which has become a proper name by the time Paul writes 2 Corinthians 6:15). Saul 'holds his peace'. In the traditional Hebrew Bible the chapter ends here, but very much on a 'to be continued' note.

4 The king is accepted   *Read 1 Samuel 10:27b–11:15*

Another story in the old style. The obvious question at the end of reading it is, How did Nahash the Ammonite keep his job? It is a bizarre tale with the usual enormous numbers and the requisite amount of gore. The Ammonite kingdom was in the highlands east of the Dead Sea (around modern Amman); Jabesh Gilead and the other places mentioned were further north on the east bank of the Jordan.

The theme words are 'deliver', 'deliverer' and 'deliverance' (10:27; 11:4, 9, 13), though NRSV uses 'save' for variety in verse 4. In the last three of these verses (v. 27 is only in the manuscript discovered at Qumran) we have the familiar words also translated as 'save', 'saviour' and 'salvation' (*soteria* in Greek and *teshua'* in Hebrew). The point is made in verse 13 that it is the Lord who delivers his people, and that it is Saul, his agent in doing it, who recognizes it.

As a result of this victory Saul's kingship is accepted and 'renewed' in a religious ceremony at another old shrine, Gilgal. Samuel had told Saul to go there and wait for him (10:8) but subsequent events had overtaken them both. Now they arrive together and all is well. Saul's magnanimity in verse 13 will be featured later in the story with very different results. The next time Saul and Samuel meet at Gilgal they will part acrimoniously with Samuel announcing the end of Saul's reign (15:10–35). All round the kingship seems a temporary and performance-related job.

Recent translations use a variety of names for the sacrifices in the ceremony : 'offerings of well-being' (NRSV), 'communion sacrifices' (NJB), 'fellowship offerings' (NIV, cf. GNB) and 'shared offerings' (REB). The older translations called them 'peace offerings', from the Hebrew word *shalom*—peace, harmony, fulfilment. These were celebratory sacrifices in which having offered part of the sacrificial animals to God the worshippers then feasted on the rest, celebrating their fellowship with God and each other.

5 Strong words from Samuel *Read 1 Samuel 12:1–25*

This long speech by Samuel adds nothing new to the argument. It does show, however, in verse 1–5, just how vulnerable leaders can feel in the lonely places of power, and how much support and encouragement they need. Here is a good text for a sermon on the need to affirm and support one another, and a preacher might even speculate on what the outcome of it all might have been if Samuel had had a support group or someone to cuddle him. For from now on Samuel himself feels increasingly threatened by what is happening and vents his feelings on Saul.

This chapter neatly encapsulates the view of the person or persons who finally put together the books of Joshua–2 Kings, whom scholars have traditionally referred to as the Deuteronomic Historian. These books illustrate the central theme of Deuteronomy that God rewards goodness with success and sin with trouble. It is vital therefore, that God's people make the right choice in life (see the classic passage which is Deuteronomy 30:15–20), but sadly they have failed to do so, and the exile is the consequence of that failure. God wants only the best for his people (and for all people) and so by reminding them of what God has done for them and warning them of the consequences of ignoring God's advice, Samuel urges them to make the right choice and live in the right way.

Note the place of repentance and forgiveness in verses 19–22 and the role of the prophet as teacher and intercessor in verse 23. 'For his name's sake' (v. 22) may mean that God is concerned for his reputation (as in Ezekiel 36:22–32): but a better understanding of the phrase is that he will act like this because it is his very nature to do so. Therefore we could paraphrase this verse by saying that he will save, because as his name is Saviour, he can do nothing else but save! To 'fear the Lord' (v. 24) is more than honouring or revering him by taking his teaching seriously; and a better modern translation of this expression would be to 'worship' him. Verses 23–25 are an excellent summary of the speech, of the teaching of the book of Deuteronomy, of the Old Testament and of the whole Bible!

6   Samuel against Saul   *Read 1 Samuel 13:1–23*

In the Hebrew text of verse 1 the number is missing from Saul's age and half a number from the length of his reign. The whole verse is missing from the Greek text. Little things like this have to be taken seriously when we think about the controversial question of the inspiration and authority of the Bible. They rule out the sort of oversimplifications about what the Bible is and how it can be used which we see in the militant fundamentalism which is such an issue in many churches today.

The real threat was not the Ammonites but the Philistines, and after an initial skirmish the Philistines muster for serious war. Saul calls the Israelite troops together, calling them 'Hebrews', a name more often used for them by others than by themselves (4:6; 13:19; 29:3). It refers to the Israelites as the descendants of Eber, who was Abraham's great, great, ever-so-great grandfather according to the genealogy in Genesis 11:16–27. It might be related to the word *Habiru*, a term used in texts from around 1000BC for bands of lawless and marginalized people who caused problems to the settled societies in the region, and if so it would be another pointer to Israel's origins.

Saul waits (v. 8), taking up the words of Samuel from 10:8 but much has happened since then. Here again is one of the seams which shows that our present story is made up of several older ones. Saul offers the sacrifices for obvious reasons. He offers the burnt-offering (a prayer of petition) but Samuel arrives before he can offer the celebratory one. We have not so far read of any such commandment as Samuel quotes, and later kings will do what Saul did without censure (2 Samuel 6:12–19; 1 Kings 3:15). What he says prepares us for Saul's failure and the choice of another king, though the following stories tell of the heroism of Saul and especially of his son.

The odds are against Israel, both in terms of numbers (vv. 15–18) and equipment (vv. 19–22, which throw interesting light on the development of technology in the region).

GUIDELINES

Readers of *Guidelines* will not, I hope, be among those who believe that the Old Testament is a book of outdated rules imposed on us by an over-demanding God. That is to miss its point and its good news, as well as to create a false opposition between the New Testament and the Old. In the Old Testament, as in the New, we read of a generous God who wants only the best for people (see especially Exodus 34:6–7 and all the places where this is echoed in the Old Testament, not least throughout Psalm 103). It is God's generosity which has rescued his oppressed people, and which then gives them advice about how to continue to make the most of their new life, as we see in the opening of the Ten Commandments (Exodus 20:2; Deuteronomy 5:6) and also in John 1:16–17. Faith is therefore an invitation to remember God's generosity and be guided by it in all of our living. Only secondarily, and then based on experience, does Bible and Church warn us of the pitfalls of trying to live otherwise. Thus 1 Samuel 12:23–25 is an excellent summary of the Bible's invitation to respond to the love which has made itself known to us. If we are still unsure, towards the end of the Decade of Evangelism, what it is that we have to say to our world then here is a reminder.

This week's chapters deal with issues of power and responsibility. No doubt the strong anti-monarchy feeling which emerges often in Samuel's speeches reflects the unfortunate experiences of the Israelites under their kings, and many before and since would echo it. Power corrupts and can so easily oppress. But the dream of everyone living peacefully and prosperously without such centralized power (which perhaps lies behind verses like Judges 17:6 and 21:25) or of everyone freely obeying God's law with the same result (as in Micah 4:1–4) is unreal. Much more practical is Psalm 72, which talks of the king's role as protector of the weak and vulnerable and which is a prayer that the king will use his power in that way. Systems of government vary, but Psalm 72 is a fine prayer for all in positions of power and responsibility.

1   A good son   *Read 1 Samuel 14:1–15*

The sons we have met so far have been bad sons of good, or at least good-enough, fathers. Now we meet Jonathan who will turn out to be a good son of a not-so-good father. Being a good son does not stop him being disobedient, prepared to act without his father's knowledge or approval (v. 1).

The story has an old and familiar theme, set out in verse 6b; but as we have already noted it is difficult to make this sort of bold statement about God's power in a world which has seen the like of Auschwitz. It tells of the victory of Israel over their enemies against overwhelming odds, achieved because the Lord fights for them. Here the odds are doubly stacked against Jonathan and his armour-bearer. Not only are they two against a garrison, but the garrison is secure in a cliff-top fort. The armour-bearer is another of the fine minor characters portrayed in the story, a model of trust, enthusiasm and reliability. Jonathan's courage, or foolhardiness, pays off.

Note that in verse 3 a great-grandson of Eli is with Saul's troops 'carrying' rather than wearing an ephod (see on 2:28, pages 130–31). In verse 6 the Philistines are scornfully called 'these uncircumcised' (compare Judges 14:3; 15:18). The origin of the practice of male circumcision in the ancient Near East is obscure. It was certainly not unique to the Israelites, for all their semitic neighbours and relatives practised it as did the Egyptians. In fact the Philistines would be the first group that the ancient Israelites met who did not, hence 'the uncircumcised' was such a handy mocking slogan. 'The Lord has given them into our hand', (v. 10) is a phrase from the Holy War traditions (compare Joshua 6:2; 8:7), in fact the name Jonathan itself means 'God has given'. 'Hands and feet' in verse 13 is too literal; 'hands and knees' as in GNB is better. Verse 14b refers either to the small area in which the slaughter took place (GNB, NIV and NRSV) or of the speed and ease with which Jonathan mowed the enemy down (REB). 'Panic', 'trembling' and 'earthquake' often feature in stories of the power of God at work (compare especially Exodus 15:14–16; Judges 5:4–5).

2 A compassionate king? *Read 1 Samuel 14:16–35*

As panic spreads among the Philistines so Saul takes advantage of it (reminiscent of the story of Gideon's victory over the Midianites in Judges 7). His troops are joined first by the Israelite mercenaries in the Philistine army and then by those who had deserted him before. We will read later of David and his men serving as mercenaries with the Philistines (1 Samuel 27:2–12, 29:1–11).

Verses 16–19 form a somewhat confused interlude. In verse 18 the Greek version refers to the ephod rather than the ark, and in verse 19 it is not clear what the priest is to withdraw his hand from. Has Saul finally seen what is happening and so no longer needs the priest to consult the Urim and Thummim in the ephod? In any case one is left wondering why Saul is dithering so much.

Verse 24 introduces an incident about an oath, reminiscent of the story of Jephthah and his daughter in Judges 11:29–40 though the outcome of this one will be very different. The NRSV follows the Greek in its reference to Saul's rash act. The Hebrew text speaks of the Israelites being 'distressed' by the hunger forced on them by Saul's curse. Jonathan, ignorant of the oath his father had made, eats the honey he finds and is greatly refreshed by it. When his error is pointed out he simply remarks that it was a silly thing for his father to have done!

At the end of the battle the troops are so hungry that they slaughter the Philistine's livestock and eat without the usual procedures for draining off the blood. According to the blood regulation in Leviticus 17:10–14 the consumption of blood, the very life of a creature, was strictly prohibited. To save his troops from sinning Saul sets up an altar so that the animals can be killed properly and due sacrifice offered for the offences already committed. Verse 35 notes in a factual way that this is his first altar, and it would not be the last one built and used by the kings who would come after him (2 Samuel 24:18–25; 1 Kings 9:25). But remembering what happened the first time he offered sacrifices (13:9–15) we are apprehensive about the consequences which will follow his good intentions here.

3 A powerful king *Read 1 Samuel 14:36–52*

Saul intends to turn the rout of the Philistines into annihilation, but Ahijah, Eli's great-grandson, proposes that God be consulted first.

Lack of an answer indicates that something is seriously wrong, and so the Urim and Thummim are used to pinpoint who is to blame. In a verse full of irony Saul swears that whoever it is will die (v. 39). Finding that it is Jonathan he repeats his oath (v. 44).

The people, showing more common sense and compassion than Saul, counter his oath with one of their own and their oath-cum-threat succeeds. Jonathan is 'ransomed' (v. 45). This may be a technical term implying that the people paid a ransom price or sacrificed an animal to free Jonathan from this oath. More likely, however, the word has no technical sense and should be translated by 'saved' (GNB, NJPS), 'rescued' (NIV), 'delivered' (REB) or the like.

The outcome is that the Philistines survive to remain a threat to Israel (v. 46), though the chapter ends with the picture of Saul as precisely the sort of successful military leader that the people had said they needed. He is personally courageous and proves to be very effective in his kingly role as protector of the Israelites against their local aggressors. In verses 49–51 we see Saul's family. No great point is made of their names, but in his three sons and two daughters there is potential for creating a dynasty. Control of the army is kept safely in the family too.

The first part of this passage makes for terrifying reading, even if we make major allowances for the story-teller sharpening it up for dramatic effect. No small part of its terror lies in the fact that there have been, and still are, in all faiths those who would see Saul at fault here for failing to honour his obligations to God. Surely a good test of any faith is to ask if it makes its practitioners sane and humane?

4 God against Saul *Read 1 Samuel 15:1–21*

The reappearance of Samuel in the story marks the beginning of the end of Saul's reign, and opens a chapter full of difficulties. God orders a holy war against the Amalekites for something that happened centuries before. They and their animals are to be 'put under the ban' (REB), i.e. totally destroyed as an offering to God (v. 3). This punishment seems all the more terrible as the Amalekites had been soundly beaten in the incident referred to anyway (Exodus 17:8–16), though it is fully in keeping with the vengeful sentiments of Deuteronomy 25:17–19. This horrendous practice was not confined to Israel; it is mentioned, for example, on the Moabite Stone erected by Mesha of Moab around 830BC to celebrate a victory over the

Israelites. However, before we condemn ancient Israelites (or Moabites) we might pause to reflect on the history of total war in our own century.

Saul musters considerably more soldiers than ever before. Once his army is in place he encourages the Kenites to escape while they can. This is their reward for helping where the Amalekites had hindered, though it is not possible to point to any specific scene in the exodus stories (v. 6). The Kenites are generally thought to have been travelling smiths or tinkers and therefore groups or families of them would have been found living among other tribes. The ensuing victory is total, but the ban is not!

Saul's fate is announced to Samuel and to us by the formal expression, 'The word of the Lord came', not heard since chapter 3 (vv. 1, 7 and 21). Samuel's reaction is anger, which he vents at God (v. 11). Many of the Psalms show that expressing anger to or at God was a feature of ancient Israelite spirituality, and it may be one from which we could learn some useful lessons. The prophet pleads with God to try to change his mind (as Moses did in Exodus 32:30–32 and Amos in 7:1–6), which is odd when we read what Samuel says in verse 29. Receiving no answer he condemns Saul for disobedience, though Saul defends himself and his motives (vv. 15 and 21).

Note verse 12. Saul sets up his own version of the Moabite Stone at nearby Carmel, not the famous mountain, but our story-teller can see nothing good in Saul now, for this stone honours himself not God (contrast 7:12).

5 Samuel and God against Saul   Read 1 Samuel 15:22–35

Samuel's reply in verses 22–23 is sometimes used as an attack on formal worship (with Isaiah 1:10–17; Hosea 6:6; Amos 5:21–24 and Micah 6:6–8 all equally taken out of context). In context it is a powerful statement about the central importance of obedience. Note the parallels and contrasts—obey and heed as opposed to rebellion and stubbornness; the seriousness of disobedience—it is equivalent to divination (REB—witchcraft), iniquity and idolatry; and the consequence of rejecting God's word is to be rejected.

Verses 24–31 raise questions about sin, confession and forgiveness. Is Saul's confession genuine or the result of emotional manipulation (contrast v. 24 with vv. 15, 20–21)? Why is there no possibility of forgiveness and a new beginning? If lessons are to be learned and principles upheld, why does Samuel help Saul to save face (vv. 30–31)? It all seems hard on Saul.

Verse 29 (compare Numbers 23:19) raises many questions by itself. It insists that God does not 'recant' or 'lie' (most translations) or 'deceive' (REB). Neither does he 'change his mind'. However, having chosen Saul and now rejected him that is precisely what he appears to be doing, and in verse 11 says he is doing! This problem is even clearer in the Hebrew where the same verb is used four times. NRSV translates it by 'regret' in verse 11, 'change his mind' twice in verse 29 and 'was sorry' in verse 35. Commentators struggle with this. God has changed his mind about Saul's kingship—but God does not change his mind! One possibility is that we read too much into verse 29. Samuel's reply to Saul might mean no more than that he has had one chance and there will not be another. In any case it is difficult to build doctrines out of stories. 'Glory of Israel' is only found here as a title for God, and the word used is not the usual word for 'glory'. In its one other association with God in the ascription of God's greatness in 1 Chronicles 29:11 it is the fourth word in the list and is translated 'victory' in the NRSV. Another translation would be 'Eternal of Israel.'

The matter-of-fact tone of the note that Samuel hewed Agag in pieces before the Lord is particularly frightening (v. 33). Despite verse 35 we find Samuel and Saul meeting again as the narrative proceeds (19:24).

6 The new Lord's Anointed *Read 1 Samuel 16:1–23*

Samuel has to put the past behind him and is instructed to anoint another king. He looks first at Jesse's eldest son, but here as so often in the Old Testament God's choice lies elsewhere. It is the youngest who is chosen. Although verse 7 notes that appearances are unimportant, verses 12 and 18 show that David had the looks as well as the character. David experiences God's powerful blessing, whereas Saul finds his blessing and well-being gone and replaced by something equally real but very nasty—'an evil spirit from the LORD'.

This expression creates difficulties for some people. How can an 'evil spirit' be said to come from God? Isaiah 45:7 gives us the clue. In the AV God says bluntly, 'I make peace and I create evil.' This verse is not, however, offering an explanation of the origins of cosmic evil. Such a question is not on the Old Testament's agenda. Isaiah 45:7 explains the woe, distress and evil which the Israelites suffered in the destruction of Jerusalem and exile to Babylon. To the question of why that happened Jeremiah, Ezekiel, Deutero-Isaiah (Isaiah 40–55) and the Deuteronomic Historian all have a simple answer: it is your own fault! You have brought your misfortune on yourselves by your own misdeeds. It is God's punishment. The same reasoning is found here. Saul is suffering severe misfortune, possibly depression. It is his own fault, God's punishment for his misdeeds. We may not be comfortable with the idea of God punishing people, but there is no doubt that the Bible doesn't share our scruples. As I have written in these Notes before, this is classic Deuteronomic and Wisdom teaching that faithfulness is rewarded and sin punished. Though it is a rather rough-and-ready, rule-of-thumb sort of doctrine, and protests against its shortcomings are found elsewhere in the Old Testament, yet is there not some truth in it?

The stories of Saul's first meeting with David are as confused as those of how Saul first became king. The picture of David in verses 11and 19 differs from the one in verse 18, and another story will have their first meeting when Goliath issues his challenge (17:19–37). Their relationship begins well. It will not end well.

GUIDELINES

Reread Samuel's words in 15:22–23. In our own discipleship there are times when this hard demand of obedience needs to be heeded, and others when what we need to hear is the different tone of Psalms 130, especially verses 3–4, or 103. Often our real difficulty is in knowing which of the two is the word from God in our particular circumstances, so prone are we to hear what we want to hear.

This week we have read of holy wars and of God's demands for total religious obedience, and seen a particularly gruesome example of the latter. Sad to say, we read similar things in our daily papers. The end of the twentieth century seems to be marked by the emergence of a militant right in all the major world faiths, a new cult of violence and nationalism and a contempt for all whose common sense or compassion prevents them from seeing things in black and white. Such was the world of Samuel, and of the one who told these stories about him.

Why read these stories in 1997? Perhaps because all human life is there; in its strength and weakness, its glory and shame, its joys and terrors. The main characters have been Samuel and Saul and they are neither heroes, nor villains. We can recognize something of ourselves in each of them, and much of our society in theirs. For me 1 Samuel 1–16 is therefore a book of warnings, raising important questions about what is a civilized society, how is it to be governed and what is the place of religion in it. It is also a book of hope, offering us the possibility of a future:

> *If you will fear the Lord and serve him and heed his voice and not rebel against the commandment of the Lord, and if both you and the king who reigns over you will follow the Lord your God, it will be well; but if you will not heed the voice of the Lord, but rebel against the commandment of the Lord, then the hand of the Lord will be against you and your king.*

1 Samuel 12:14–15

For further reading

P.R. Ackroyd, *1 Samuel*, Cambridge Bible Commentary, CUP

G. Auld, *1 and 2 Samuel*, Daily Study Bible, St Andrew Press

Guidelines © BRF 1997

The Bible Reading Fellowship
Peter's Way, Sandy Lane West, Oxford, OX4 5HG
ISBN 0 7459 3534 6

Distributed in Australia by:
Albatross Books Pty Ltd, PO Box 320, Sutherland,
NSW 2232

Distributed in New Zealand by:
Scripture Union Wholesale, PO Box 760, Wellington

Distributed in South Africa by:
Struik Book Distributors, PO Box 193, Maitland 7405

Publications distributed to more than 60 countries

Acknowledgments
The Revised Standard Version of the Bible, copyright ©
1946, 1952, 1971 by the Division of Christian Education
of the National Council of the Churches of Christ in the
USA.

The New Revised Standard Version of the Bible, copyright ©
1989 by the Division of Christian Education of the
National Council of the Churches of Christ in the USA.

The Holy Bible, New International Version, copyright ©
1973, 1978, 1984 by International Bible Society. Used
by permission of Hodder & Stoughton Ltd.

Cover photograph: Lion Publishing

Printed in Denmark

ORDER FORMS

SUBSCRIPTIONS

☐ I would like to give a gift subscription (please complete both name and address sections below)

☐ I would like to take out a subscription myself (complete name and address details only once)

☐ Please send me details of 3- and 5-year subscriptions

This completed coupon should be sent with appropriate payment to BRF. Alternatively, please write to us quoting your name, address, the subscription you would like for either yourself or a friend (with their name and address), the start date and credit card number, expiry date and signature if paying by credit card.

Gift subscription name _____

Gift subscription address _____

_____

_____ Postcode _____

Please send to the above, beginning with the May/September 1997 issue:

(please tick box)	UK	SURFACE	AIR MAIL
LIVEWIRES	☐ £12.00	☐ £13.50	☐ £15.00
GUIDELINES	☐ £9.30	☐ £10.50	☐ £12.90
NEW DAYLIGHT	☐ £9.30	☐ £10.50	☐ £12.90
NEW DAYLIGHT LARGE PRINT	☐ £15.00	☐ £18.60	☐ £21.00

Please complete the payment details below and send your coupon, with appropriate payment to: **The Bible Reading Fellowship, Peter's Way, Sandy Lane West, Oxford OX4 5HG**

Your name _____

Your address _____

_____

_____ Postcode _____

Total enclosed £ _____ (cheques should be made payable to 'BRF')

Payment by cheque ☐ postal order ☐ Visa ☐ Mastercard ☐ Switch ☐

Card number: ☐☐☐☐ ☐☐☐☐ ☐☐☐☐ ☐☐☐☐

Expiry date of card: ☐☐☐☐   Issue number (Switch): ☐☐☐☐

Signature (essential if paying by credit/Switch card) _____

NB: BRF notes are also available from your local Christian bookshop.

GL0297   The Bible Reading Fellowship is a Registered Charity

BIBLE READING RESOURCES PACK

A pack of resources and ideas to help to promote Bible reading in your church is available from BRF. The pack which will be of use at any time during the year includes sample editions of the notes, magazine articles, leaflets about BRF Bible reading resources and much more. Unless you specify the month in which you would like the pack sent, we will send it immediately on receipt of your order. We greatly appreciate your donations towards the cost of producing the pack (without them we would not be able to make the pack available) and we welcome your comments about the contents of the pack and your ideas for future ones.

This coupon should be sent to:

The Bible Reading Fellowship
Peter's Way
Sandy Lane West
Oxford OX4 5HG

Name _____

Address _____

_____

_____ Postcode _____

Please send me _____ Bible Reading Resources Pack(s)

Please send the pack now/ in_____ (month).

I enclose a donation for £_____ towards the cost of the pack.

The Bible Reading Fellowship is a Registered Charity

GL0297

BRF PUBLICATIONS ORDER FORM

Please ensure that you complete and send off both sides of this order form.

Please send me the following book(s):

		Quantity	Price	Total
2526	Time to Change (H. Montefiore)	_____	£6.99	_____
3516	Connecting with God (J. Levermore)	_____	£5.99	_____
2522	Visions of Love (W. Sykes)	_____	£10.99	_____
2591	Visions of Hope (W. Sykes)	_____	£10.99	_____
2977	Visions of Glory (W. Sykes)	_____	£9.99	_____
3098	Visions of Faith (W. Sykes)	_____	£10.99	_____
3503	Visions of Grace (W. Sykes)	_____	£11.99	_____
3509	The Jesus Prayer (S. Barrington-Ward)	_____	£3.50	_____
3253	The Matthew Passion (J. Fenton)	_____	£5.99	_____
3295	Livewires: Footsteps and Fingerprints (R. Sharples)	_____	£3.50	_____
3296	Livewires: Families and Feelings (H. Butler)	_____	£3.50	_____
3522	Livewires: Friends and Followers (S. Herbert)	_____	£3.50	_____
3523	Livewires: Tiptoes and Fingertips (B. Ogden)	_____	£3.50	_____
2821	People's Bible Commentary: Genesis (H. Wansbrough)	_____	£5.99	_____
2824	People's Bible Commentary: Mark (R.T. France)	_____	£7.99	_____
3281	People's Bible Commentary: Galatians (J. Fenton)	_____	£4.99	_____
2531	Sowers and Reapers (ed. J Parr)	_____	£9.99	_____
3250	Prophets and Poets (ed. G. Emmerson)	_____	£8.99	_____

FEATURED BOOKS · **LIVEWIRES** · **PBC** · **GENERAL**

Total cost of books £ _____

Postage and packing (see over) £ _____

TOTAL £ _____

See over for payment details. All prices are correct at time of going to press, are subject to the prevailing rate of VAT and may be subject to change without prior warning.

NB: All BRF titles are also available from your local Christian bookshop.

GL0297   The Bible Reading Fellowship is a Registered Charity

PAYMENT DETAILS

Please complete the payment details below and send with appropriate payment and completed order form to:

The Bible Reading Fellowship,
Peter's Way,
Sandy Lane West,
Oxford OX4 5HG

Name _____

Address _____

_____

_____ Postcode _____

Total enclosed £ _____ (cheques should be made payable to 'BRF')

Payment by cheque ☐ postal order ☐ Visa ☐ Mastercard ☐ Switch ☐

Card number: ☐☐☐☐ ☐☐☐☐ ☐☐☐☐ ☐☐☐☐

Expiry date of card: ☐☐☐☐   Issue number (Switch): ☐☐☐☐

Signature (essential if paying by credit/Switch card) _____

POSTAGE AND PACKING CHARGES			
order value	UK	Europe	Surface	Air Mail
£6.00 & under	£1.25	£2.25	£2.25	£3.50
£6.01–£14.99	£3.00	£3.50	£4.50	£6.50
£15.00–£29.99	£4.00	£5.50	£7.50	£11.00
£30.00 & over	free	prices on request		

Alternatively you may wish to order books using the BRF telephone order hotline:
01865 748227